How to Prepare For the CAT/6*

teacher

* CAT/ 6 is a registered trademark of Educational Testing Service, which was not involved in the production of and does not endorse this product

1st Grade Edition

By Nancy Samuels

carney
EDUCATIONAL SERVICES

CARNEY EDUCATIONAL SERVICES
Helping Students Help Themselves

Special thanks to Rim Namkoong, our illustrator

This book is dedicated to:

The moms and dads who get up early and stay up late. You are the true heroes, saving our future, one precious child at a time.

All the kids who don't make the evening news. To the wide-eyed children, full of love, energy, and wonder. You are as close to perfection as this world will ever see.

TABLE OF CONTENTS

Introduction for Parents

The Focus and Purpose of this Book

California recently adopted rigorous academic content standards for students in grades K – 12. The content standards set forth exactly what students need to learn in each grade level in language arts, mathematics, history-social science, and science. This book presents exercises that test student mastery of each of the academic content standards.

In conjunction with the standards, California initiated the Standardized Testing and Reporting (STAR) program. As a part of the STAR program, students take the nationally normed California Achievement Test (CAT/6) and the California Standards Tests designed by the state to assess how well the students have mastered the skills and information covered in the language arts and mathematics content standards.[1] The results give teachers, parents, and students invaluable information about a child's relative academic strengths and the next steps for learning. (For more information about the STAR program, visit the California Department of Education website at http://www.cde.ca.gov.)

The purpose of this book is twofold: (1) to assist students in mastering the information addressed in each of the content standards, and (2) to prepare students to perform their best on the STAR. It is designed for student use in the classroom or for support of classroom lessons. The book is divided into "practice skill" sections that correlate to the various strands of the content standards. Each section is introduced with a statement of expectations for student learning in the practice skill area. Every section also contains tips and strategies to help the student learn the information or reason through the exercises. The exercises are presented in various formats that will give the students practice in answering questions much like those that they are likely to encounter on any standardized nationally normed test.

The California Academic Content Standards in Grade 1

By the end of grade 1, students are expected to achieve mastery in several areas. The major areas of focus are listed below.

LANGUAGE ARTS areas of focus include:
- Word Analysis, Fluency, and Systematic Vocabulary Development
    - Match oral words to printed words
    - Identify letters, words, and sentences
    - Distinguish initial, medial, and final sounds in words
    - Distinguish long- and short-vowel sounds in orally stated words
    - Change target sounds to change words (change *cow* to *how*)
    - Create a series of rhyming words
    - Blend phonemes into recognizable words (/c/a/t/ = cat)
    - Segment words into their components (cat = /c/a/t)

---

[1] As part of the STAR, students in grades 4 and 7 also take a timed test of writing proficiency. In this test, students are given a prompt and asked to write a persuasive essay, a descriptive piece, a story (narrative), or an expository essay.

Language Arts, Continued

- o Generate the sounds from all the letters and letter patterns, and blend them into words
- o Read common, irregular sight words (e.g., *the, have, said, come, give, of*)
- o Read compound words and contractions
- o Read inflectional forms and root words
- o Read common word families
- o Read aloud with fluency in a manner that sounds like natural speech
- Reading Comprehension
  - o Identify the organizational structure of text
  - o Respond to *who, what, when, where*, and *how* questions
  - o Follow one-step written instructions
  - o Use context to resolve ambiguities about word and sentence meanings
  - o Confirm predictions about what will happen next in a text by identifying key words
  - o Retell the central ideas of simple expository or narrative passages
- Literary Response and Analysis
  - o Identify plot, setting, and character in a story, as well as the story's beginning, middle, and ending
  - o Describe the roles of authors and illustrators of print material
  - o Recollect, talk and write about books read during the school year
- Listening and Speaking
  - o Listen attentively and ask questions for clarification and explanation
  - o Give, restate, and follow two-step directions
  - o Stay on topic when speaking
  - o Use descriptive words when speaking
  - o Recite poems, songs, and stories
  - o Retell stories in sequence by answering *who, what, when, where, why* and *how* questions
  - o Relate an important personal experience in sequence
  - o Provide descriptions with careful attention to sensory detail
- Writing Strategies and Applications
  - o Write complete, coherent sentences
  - o Select a focus when writing
  - o Use descriptive words when writing
  - o Print legibly and space letters, words, and sentences appropriately
  - o Write brief narratives describing a fictional or autobiographical experience
  - o Write brief expository descriptions of a real object, person, place, or event, using sensory details
- Written and Oral English Language Conventions
  - o Write and speak in complete, coherent sentences
  - o Correctly use singular and plural nouns, contractions, and singular possessive pronouns in writing and speaking
  - o Properly punctuate declarative, exclamatory, and interrogative sentences
  - o Use the basic rules of punctuation and capitalization when writing
  - o Spell three- and four-letter short-vowel words and grade-level-appropriate sight words correctly

MATHEMATICS areas of focus include:
- Number Sense
    - Count, read, and write whole numbers to 100
    - Compare and order whole numbers using the symbols >, <, or =
    - Count and group objects in ones and tens
    - Identify and know the value of coins and show different combinations of coins that equal the same value
    - Know the addition facts (sums to 20) and the corresponding subtraction facts
    - Use the inverse relationship between addition and subtraction to solve problems
    - Count by 2s, 5s, and 10s to 100
    - Solve addition and subtraction problems with one- and two-digit numbers
    - Find the sum of three one-digit numbers
    - Use estimation strategies in computation and problem solving
- Algebra and Functions
    - Use number sentences involving addition and subtraction to solve problems
- Measurement and Geometry
    - Measure objects using direct comparison and nonstandard units
    - Tell time to the nearest half hour
    - Identify, describe and compare triangles, rectangles, squares, and circles
- Statistics, Data Analysis, and Probability
    - Organize, represent, and compare data by category on simple graphs and charts
    - Explain ways to get to a next element in simple repeating patterns
- Mathematical Reasoning
    - Make decisions about how to set up a problem; use appropriate problem solving strategies
    - Make precise calculations and check the validity of the results

HISTORY-SOCIAL SCIENCE areas of focus include:
- A Child's Place in Time and Space
    - Describe the rights and individual responsibilities of citizenship
    - Understand the elements of fair play and good sportsmanship
    - Describe how location, weather, and physical environment affect people's lives
    - Study transportation methods of earlier days
    - Recognize similarities and differences of earlier generations in various aspects of our culture
    - Examine the structure of schools and communities in the past
- Map Skills
    - Locate on maps and globes their country, state, and community
    - Locate on maps and globes the seven continents and four oceans
    - Construct a map using cardinal directions and map symbols

History-Social Science, Continued
- Symbols, Icons, and Traditions of the U.S., and Concepts of Character
  - Recite the Pledge of Allegiance and sing patriotic songs
  - Understand the significance of our national holidays and the heroism and achievements of the people associated with them
  - Identify American symbols, landmarks, and essential documents, and know the people and events associated with them
- Cultural Diversity
  - Recognize the forms of diversity in school and community
  - Understand the ways in which America's native peoples and immigrants have helped define Californian and American culture
  - Compare the beliefs, customs, ceremonies, traditions, and social practices of the varied cultures, drawing from folklore
- Economic Concepts
  - Understand the concepts of exchange and the use of money to purchase goods and services
  - Identify the specialized work that people do to manufacture, transport, and market goods and services and the contributions of those who work in the home

SCIENCE areas of focus include:
- Physical Sciences
  - Know that solids, liquids, and gases have different properties
  - Know that the properties of substances can change when the substances are mixed, cooled, or heated
- Life Sciences
  - Know that different plants and animals inhabit different kinds of environments and have external features that help them thrive
  - Know that both plants and animals need water, animals need food, and plants need light.
  - Know the role of producers and consumers
  - Know the basic parts of plants and their functions
- Earth Sciences
  - Know the ways that weather can be observed, measured, and described
  - Know the predictable changes in weather related to the seasons
- Investigation and Experimentation
  - Develop questions and perform investigations
  - Record observations on a bar graph

Test Taking Strategies for Students in Grade 1

Students in grade 1 receive their own test booklets in which to read the questions and fill in a bubble next to their answer choice. The bubbling marks are the only ones that they will be allowed to make on the tests. For the math sections, however, students may use scratch paper. No calculators are allowed. In fact, to ensure the integrity of the testing, during the testing period teachers must remove all charts and diagrams relevant to the subject of the test.

►Listen Carefully, Bubble Accurately, and Keep Up With the Pace

An important aspect of the test is that a student must listen carefully and pay close attention to the teacher before, during, and after the test. The teacher will give oral instructions about the test and will read parts of the test to the students. The teacher's words are scripted, and the script sets strict limits on the number of times instructions and test questions may be repeated. A student must remain attentive, keep track of the number of the question that they are answering, and make sure to keep up with the pace.

►Eliminate Any Unreasonable Answer Choices and Select the Best Answer

In a test with a multiple-choice format, it is sometimes difficult to find the "perfect" answer among the choices given. First, eliminate all obviously wrong choices in order to concentrate on the remaining ones. Ultimately, it may be difficult to choose between two choices. In such instances, the student should reread the question carefully. It will likely contain key words needed to select the best answer. It may be the case that two choices are factually correct, but one choice more directly answers the question than another. Consider the following example:

Read the passage and answer the question about it.

Dogs are members of the canine family. They come in a variety of breeds and hundreds of different shapes and sizes. Each breed has its own special talent. Sheep dogs herd cows and sheep. Golden retrievers and German shepherds make good guide dogs for the blind. St. Bernards are famous for finding people who are lost in the mountains. Huskies pull sleds to transport people and supplies over snow.

1. What is the main idea of this selection?

      a. All dogs are canines.
      b. All dogs look the same.
      c. Dogs make good friends.
      d. Different dog breeds have special jobs and talents.

To select the best answer, first eliminate the obviously incorrect choice "b." Although the remaining choices are all true statements, and even though choice "a" is taken directly from the selection, only choice "d" addresses the main idea of the passage. Choice "d" is the best answer.

►Solve Math Problems on Scratch Paper. Work Neatly and Keep Organized.

       Students may not make marks in the test booklet, except to bubble in their answers. Teachers will distribute scratch paper for solving problems. It will be important to transfer the problem accurately onto the scratch paper, align columns, and keep track of what problem is being solved. This means that the student will need to pay extra attention to neatness, organization, and accuracy. Time is often a factor in math tests, so it is will be necessary to work steadily and focus on the task at hand. If the student is really stumped on one problem, it may be best to give an educated guess, make a notation about the problem number, and return to it later if time permits. Any questions left unanswered will be counted wrong, so it is best not too spend too much time on any one problem. There is probably a question waiting down the line that will be much easier to solve!

Introduction for Students

About This Book

The state of California has developed a set of guidelines (called "academic content standards") for students in every grade, from Kindergarten through grade 12. These standards tell us exactly what students need to learn in each grade level in language arts, math, history-social science (social studies), and science. The exercises in this book follow the standards for first grade. As you complete these exercises, you will be able to tell which standards you have learned and which areas you might want to review.

In order to know how well children are learning the information they need to know, many students in California take certain tests every year in the spring. The exercises in this book will help you get ready for these tests. They will give you practice in answering questions about the things that you will need to know by the end of first grade.

This book is divided into four sections, one for each of the subjects where there are established standards: language arts, math, history-social science, and science. Each section is divided into practice skill areas that explain what students are expected to know under the particular standard. Look for the box of tips in each section. The tips will explain special ways to remember the information, or will give you help in working through the exercises.

What You Will Learn in the First Grade

In the first grade you will accomplish many things. Here are some of them:

Language Arts - You will read silently and read aloud with understanding. You will learn the meaning of many new words. You will analyze poetry, stories, and books that give you new information. You will organize your thoughts to speak and write in a way that is clear to others.

Math – You will work with numbers from 1 to 100 and add and subtract numbers. You will measure, describe data, and analyze and solve simple problems.

History-Social Studies – The theme for the year is "A Child's Place in Time and Space." You will study the rules by which we all must live. You will compare and contrast your life with the lives of others who live in different places or lived in different times. You will learn more about the United States and the world around you.

Science – One area of focus is the study of solids, liquids, and gases. You will also learn about what plants and animals need to stay alive in different environments. First grade students also study the weather. In learning about these topics, you will question, observe, predict, investigate, experiment, and record data. You will be a scientist!

Test Taking Tips

1.   **Read for 20 minutes every day.** The skills that you use to read are the same skills that will help you to do well on any test.

2.   **Review a little every day.** If you practice or review what you have already learned in class, it will help you to remember the information when it appears on a test. It is easier to learn and practice something in six 10-minute sessions than in one hour-long session.

3.   **When solving math problems, work neatly and keep organized.** Take extra care when you are writing problems or transferring answers from scratch paper to a test booklet. You must copy the problems accurately and compute accurately. It helps to work each problem in its own area, separated from another problem. Be sure to align columns correctly. This will help you to avoid careless errors.

4.   **Stay focused.** Often, you will only have a limited time to complete a test. Other times you will need to listen to your teacher's instructions or respond to what you hear. Be sure to concentrate on the task at hand. Keep working and don't let your mind wander. If you don't know an answer, be sure not to spend so much time on that one question that you can't finish the rest of the test. Consider taking an educated guess or skipping the question and coming back to work on it after you have completed the rest of the test.

5.   **In multiple-choice tests, eliminate obviously wrong choices and select the best answer.** Sometimes it is difficult to find the "perfect" answer among the choices given. The first thing to do is eliminate the choices that are obviously wrong and concentrate on the remaining ones. If you find it difficult to choose between two choices that both seem correct, go back and reread the question very carefully. Look for key words that will help you focus on the best choice. Don't be fooled by choices that are true, but that do not directly answer the question! Here is an example:

Read the passage and answer the question about it.

There are many kinds of dogs. They come in hundreds of different shapes and sizes. Each breed has its own special talent. Sheep dogs herd cows and sheep. Golden retrievers make good guide dogs for the blind. St. Bernards are famous for finding people who are lost in the mountains. Huskies pull sleds to carry people and packages over ice and snow.

1. What is the main idea of this selection?

    a. Sheep dogs herd cows and sheep.
    b. All dogs look the same.
    c. Dogs make good pets.
    d. Different dog breeds have special jobs and talents.

To select the best answer, first eliminate the obviously incorrect choice "b." Although the remaining choices are all true statements, and even though choice "a" is stated in the paragraph, only choice "d" tells the main idea of the paragraph. Choice "d" is the correct answer.

6.   **Take some practice tests so you won't be nervous.** The more you get used to thinking about what you know and answering questions about it, the more comfortable and confident you can be. A positive attitude is always the best way to approach learning and testing. The exercises in this book are designed to help you learn what you need to know in first grade and to practice answering questions about it. You will be able to say, "I know how to do this. I do it all the time!"

NOTES

LANGUAGE ARTS

Practice Skill: READING COMPREHENSION

Expectation: Be a careful and accurate reader. Think about what you are reading. Keep asking yourself, "Does this make sense?"

> Tip: Good readers think about what they are reading. When they read something new, they look at pictures, titles, and key words to get an idea about what they will read. When they come to a word they don't know, they think of words that will make sense, and they try again. They use the rest of the words to help figure out the one they don't know.

Exercise # 1 - Read the sentence or sentences. Find the word that makes sense in the blank.

Example:　I have a _____ that I want to read.

      a.　　fish
      b.　　book
      c.　　cow
      d.　　cat

    First, read the sentence and say "*Mmmm*" at the blank. Then read the sentence again substituting each choice in the blank. Each time ask yourself, "Does this make sense?" In this example, think, "I have a *Mmmm* that I want to read." Then think, "I have a *fish* that I want to read." Do the same thing with the next choices. "I have a *book* that I want to read. I have a *cow* that I want to read. I have a *cat* that I want to read." Be sure to read all of the choices. The correct answer is choice *b*.

1. We went to the zoo to see the _____.

    a. forks
    b. apples
    c. elephants
    d. moon

2. Tia saw some _____ at the beach.

    a. shells
    b. dinosaurs
    c. sad
    d. push

3. The _____ keeps the beat of the music.

    a. nest
    b. drip
    c. draw
    d. drum

4. The fastest way to get to get across the lake is by _____.

    a. boat
    b. walk
    c. bird
    d. mail

5. The bird _____ from tree to tree.

    a. grew
    b. flew
    c. spit
    d. fried

6. The last one out of the _____ must turn off the lights.

    a. smell
    b. smile
    c. room
    d. friend

7. It was so hot outside that I wore my _____.

    a. baseball
    b. rainboots
    c. gloves
    d. T-shirt

8. Have you ever tried to grow a _____ from a seed?

    a. plant
    b. purple
    c. purse
    d. picture

9. I hope it does not rain. I _____ my umbrella.

    a. for
    b. form
    c. forgot
    d. food

10. My bedroom was such a _____ that I stayed inside to clean it up.

    a. mail
    b. might
    c. meat
    d. mess

11. Will you have a _____ on your birthday?

    a. person
    b. pencil
    c. paper
    d. party

12. I was so _____ today that I ate a snack.

    a. hurt
    b. hungry
    c. hunted
    d. hear

13. Did you _____ your homework back to school?

   a. brew
   b. bright
   c. bring
   d. blue

14. Do you like to make _____ in the winter?

   a. snowballs
   b. butterflies
   c. toothpicks
   d. cardboard

15. My best _____ and I eat lunch together every day.

   a. fish
   b. friend
   c. firm
   d. flip

16. When I heard the _____, I turned around.

   a. roof
   b. new
   c. noise
   d. cool

17. The baby took a nap in her _____.

   a. crayon
   b. crown
   c. crib
   d. crust

18. He _____ over the fence to get the ball.

   a. clipped
   b. cleaned
   c. kite
   d. climbed

Exercise # 2 - Read the selection. Then choose the best answer to each question.

My name is Sarina. I am in the first grade. My brother, Sol, is in grade four. He tells me funny stories about when he was in the first grade. We laugh a lot. Sol reads with me every day after school. He helps me learn new words.

1. Who is in the first grade?

   a. Susan
   b. Sol
   c. Sarina
   d. Sarina's sister

2. Why does Sarina laugh?

   a. She likes to tell jokes.
   b. Sol tells her funny stories.
   c. Sol will not read to her.
   d. It does not say.

3. How does Sol help Sarina?

   a. He takes her to the store.
   b. He does her homework for her.
   c. He helps her to read new words.
   d. It does not say.

4. When do Saul and Sarina read?

   a. They only read at school.
   b. They read every day after school.
   c. They read every day before school.
   d. It does not say.

5. Who is telling the story?

   a. Sol
   b. Sarina
   c. Sarina's brother
   d. It does not say.

Exercise # 3 - The following information tells about a book. Read the information and answer the questions.

HOW TO BE HAPPY EVERY DAY

by Mary W. Lee
Illustrated by John Green

Table of Contents

Chapter 1	Be Happy at Home	Page 1
	Moms, Dads, Sisters, and Brothers	Page 5
Chapter 2	Be Happy at School	Page 8
	Know the Rules	Page 9
	Playground Games	Page 10
Chapter 3	Friends	Page 12
	Making New Friends	Page 13
	Keeping Old Friends	Page 15
Chapter 4	Rain, Rain, Go Away	Page 17
	Ways to Make Your Own Fun	Page 18

Example A: What is the title of the book?

    a. <u>Be Happy At Home</u>
    b. Mary W. Lee
    c. <u>How To Be Happy Every Day</u>
    d. Table of Contents

The correct answer is *c*. The title of the book is usually found at the top of the first page. The other choices are incorrect because they refer to the author (choice *b*), a chapter title (choice *a*), or the page title (choice *d*).

1. Chapter 4 begins on page _____.

    a. 1
    b. 12
    c. 17
    d. 18

2. Where can you read about things to do on a rainy day?

    a. Chapter 1
    b. Chapter 2
    c. Chapter 3
    d. Chapter 4

3. Who is the author of the book?

    a. Mary W. Green
    b. John Green
    c. Mary W. Lee
    d. It does not say.

4. Who drew the pictures for the book?

    a. Mary W. Lee
    b. John Green
    c. Mary W. Lee and John Green
    d. It does not say.

5. If you want to meet your new neighbor and you don't know how, read

    a. page 13.
    b. page 7.
    c. page 17.
    d. page 9.

6. If you want to look up the rules for hopscotch or kickball, turn to

    a. page 17.
    b. page 1.
    c. page 5.
    d. page 10.

Exercise # 4 - Read the story. Choose the best answer for each question.

Cole loves the circus. Uncle Rudy takes him to see the show every year. The clowns are so funny that Cole laughs until he cries. Uncle Rudy enjoys the man who jumps rope while standing on top of a galloping horse. But they both agree that their favorite act is Leona, the lion tamer. She plays with the huge tigers and lions like they are her house pets. Cole and Uncle Rudy think Leona is very brave.

1. What is this story mostly about?

   a. Uncle Rudy
   b. Cole
   c. circus acts that are fun to watch
   d. why Cole cries at the circus

2. Who is Leona?

   a. Cole's mother
   b. the funniest clown
   c. the lion tamer
   d. the galloping horse

3. Why does Cole cry?

   a. He laughs so hard at the clowns.
   b. The clowns make him very sad.
   c. He does not want to go to the circus.
   d. He does not want to leave the circus.

4. When do Cole and Uncle Rudy go to the circus?

   a. every summer
   b. every month
   c. every year
   d. The story does not say.

5. What is Cole's favorite part of the show?

   a. the elephants
   b. the clowns
   c. the horse
   d. the lion tamer

6. Which sentence is true?

    a. The clowns are sad.
    b. Uncle Rudy wants a pet tiger.
    c. This was Cole's first trip to the circus.
    d. Cole has been to the circus before.

7. What do Cole and Uncle Rudy think about the lion tamer?

    a. He is funny.
    b. He is crazy.
    c. He is brave.
    d. None of the above

8. What does Uncle Rudy think about the clowns?

    a. He thinks they are funny.
    b. The story does not say.
    c. They are better than the lion tamer.
    d. They are not as funny as the dancing bear.

9. Who jumps rope?

    a. Leona
    b. the galloping horse
    c. the clowns
    d. none of the above

10. Which sentence is true?

    a. Cole loves the circus.
    b. Cole loves the circus more than Uncle Rudy.
    c. Cole wants to be a lion tamer when he grows up.
    d. Uncle Rudy's favorite act is the horse who jumps rope.

Exercise # 5 - Read the following selection. Choose the best answer for each question.

Nothing tastes better than lemonade on a hot day. It's easy to make. Give it a try!

First, wash two lemons. Use a plastic knife to cut the lemons in half and poke out the seeds. Now squeeze the lemon juice into a glass. Add a teaspoon of sugar. Pour water into the glass to fill it up. Stir it with a spoon and then take a sip. If it is too sour, add a little more sugar to sweeten it a bit, or just drink it up and let your lips pucker.

1. What is a good title for this selection?

    a. How to Build a Lemonade Stand
    b. How to Make Lemonade
    c. Lemons Are Sour
    d. Making Lemonade is Hard to Do

2. How does the writer present the information?

    a. The first paragraph tells the reader exactly what is needed to make lemonade.
    b. The writer tells the reader how to make lemonade one step at a time.
    c. There is no order to the paragraphs.
    d. The writer does not tell the reader what to do first.

3. What do you need to make lemonade?

    a. lemons, water, sugar
    b. lemons, glass, salt
    c. spoon, glass, bowl
    d. none of the above

4. Why would you take a sip of the lemonade?

    a. to save all the lemons
    b. because you are very thirsty
    c. to see if it is sweet
    d. because you are scared

5. After you cut the lemon, what do you use the knife to do?

    a. wash the lemons
    b. stir the lemon juice in the water
    c. poke out the seeds
    d. cut the lemon

6. When does the author like to drink lemonade?
    a. on a hot day
    b. on a cold day
    c. every night
    d. with a dish of ice cream

7. What does the author like better than the taste of lemonade on a hot day?

    a. popsicles
    b. ice cream
    c. sugar
    d. nothing

8. When will your lips pucker?

    a. when the drink is too sweet
    b. when the drink is too sour
    c. when the drink tastes just right
    d. none of the above

Exercise # 6 - Read the following selection. Choose the best answer to each question.

Sara and her brother had waited weeks for this day to come. They took their baseball gloves, grabbed the tickets, and jumped in the car. Their father drove them to the ball park. They ate hot dogs and ice cream as they watched the game. After the home team won, there were fireworks in the evening sky. It was a day they would remember for many years.

1. Where did Sara and her brother go?

   a. to a baseball game
   b. to a football game
   c. to a birthday party
   d. on vacation

2. What word best describes how Sara and her brother felt about the day?

   a. tired
   b. silly
   c. excited
   d. confused

3. What did they do at the game?

   a. caught a fly ball.
   b. talked to the pitcher
   c. forgot the tickets
   d. none of the above

4. Who took Sara to the game?

   a. her brother
   b. her mother
   c. her father
   d. none of the above

5. What part of the story tells you the game ended in the night?

   a. They ate hot dogs and ice cream.
   b. They drove in the car.
   c. There were fireworks in the evening sky.
   d. None of the above

Exercise # 7 - Read the following selection. Choose the best answer to each question.

Every year before Mavis goes back to school in September, she visits her Grandma May. Grandma May lives in the country. Life on the farm is hard work, but Grandma May always makes sure that she and Mavis have fun together. First, they pick apples off the trees. Then they cook them to make applesauce. They usually have enough left over to make a delicious dessert. This year, Grandma taught Mavis how to bake the apples with sugar and cinnamon on top. It is a yummy treat. Next year, Grandma and Mavis plan to make apple juice and apple butter. Mavis will bring some home to her friends in the city.

1. Where does Grandma live?

    a. on a ranch in the country
    b. near an airport
    c. in the city
    d. on a farm in the country

2. Who lives in the city?

    a. Grandma
    b. Mavis
    c. Mavis and her friends
    d. None of the above

3. What do Mavis and Grandma do first?

    a. cook applesauce
    b. bake apples
    c. make apple juice
    d. pick apples from the trees

4. What did Grandma teach Mavis this year?

    a. to make baked apples
    b. to make apple juice
    c. to make apple pie
    d. none of the above

5. When does Mavis visit her grandmother?

    a. in May
    b. before school starts
    c. after school starts in September
    d. when the apple blossoms appear

6. Every year, what do Mavis and Grandma May make?

    a. apple pie
    b. apple juice
    c. applesauce
    d. apple butter

7. Which sentence is true?

    a. Grandma loves apple juice.
    b. Mavis has friends who live in the city.
    c. Mavis does not enjoy her farm visits.
    d. Mavis and Grandma buy apples at the store.

8. How does Mavis get to the farm?

    a. by car
    b. by train
    c. by airplane
    d. It does not say.

9. Where does Mavis usually live?

    a. in the country
    b. in the city
    c. in another state
    d. It does not say

Exercise # 8 - Read the following selection. Choose the best answer to each question.

Americans love ice cream. In fact, every year, ice cream makers will sell almost 5 gallons for every man, woman, and child in the U.S.! That's a lot of vanilla, chocolate, and strawberry (the flavors that sell the best). But have you ever tasted fancy flavors like bubble gum or spaghetti with cheese and garlic? What about dinosaur fudge? Don't let the name fool you. No dinosaur ever tasted ice cream!

We are not sure who made the first ice cream, but people tell interesting stories that might be true. Some people say that seven hundred years ago, Marco Polo learned how to make ice cream when he went to China. Then, when he came home to Italy, he put fruit and honey in snow. Other people say that four hundred years ago, King Charles I of England had a cook who made a special treat for the king. It was a sweet frozen cream. The king loved it so much that he wanted to keep it just for his own parties. He paid his cook a lot of money not to tell other cooks how to make it. For many years, ice cream was the king's secret.

In America, Thomas Jefferson and George Washington had "cold rooms" where they kept snow at their homes. They both had ice cream machines. The White House has served ice cream since 1813. In 1984, President Reagan made July "ice cream month" in America. But even in the winter, Americans love ice cream.

1. What is a good title for this selection?

    a. How to Make Ice Cream
    b. My Favorite Flavor is Chocolate
    c. Ice Cream in America
    d. Desserts

2. Which sentence is true?

    a. Winter is "ice cream month" in America.
    b. King Charles told everyone about ice cream.
    c. The dinosaurs even ate ice cream.
    d. None of the above

3. What flavors sell the best?

   a. bubble gum and peanut butter
   b. chocolate chip and mint
   c. vanilla, chocolate, and strawberry
   d. spaghetti with cheese and garlic

4. Who wanted to keep ice cream a secret?

   a. George Washington
   b. Thomas Jefferson
   c. Marco Polo
   d. King Charles I

5. According to some stories, the first ice cream was made seven hundred years ago in _____.

   a. China
   b. Italy
   c. England
   d. America

6. When was ice cream first served in the White House?

   a. 1984
   b. 1813
   c. Seven hundred years ago
   d. It does not say.

7. If you want to know how much milk it takes to make a gallon of ice cream,

   a. you must read another article.
   b. you can find it in this selection.
   c. you can ask your pet cow.
   d. none of the above

8. If you want to know which month is "ice cream month" in America,

   a. you must read another article.
   b. you can find it in this selection.
   c. you can ask your pet cow.
   d. none of the above

Practice Skill: LITERARY RESPONSE AND ANALYSIS

Expectations: Identify the plot, setting, and characters in a story. Describe the beginning, middle, and ending of a story.

Tip: As you read a story, it is important to spot some important ideas. Here is what to look for.

Characters

Who is in the story?

What kind of personalities do they have?

Do their attitudes change throughout the story?

Setting

Where does the story take place?

Does the place where the characters live affect them?

Problem and Trying to Solve the Problem (The Plot)

What happens to the characters?

What are the main events in the story?

Resolution or Conclusion

How is the problem solved?

As you discover these things about the story, think about other stories you have read that have similar or different plots and characters.

Read the following short story. Then choose the best answer to each question.

Jake and his older sister, Kate, were walking home from school one day. They were almost home when they noticed a fluffy white dog with long hair and short legs following behind them. They stopped. He stopped. They walked. He walked, too. They talked. The little white dog barked.

"Where did he come from?" Kate said out loud. "He's so cute. He must belong to somebody who lives near here."

"He just showed up. I do not see a collar on him. Let's bring him home with us," said Jake.

"No way, Jake. Mom will have a fit! Just keep walking and don't look back," Kate warned.

"Ruff, ruff!" barked the little white dog. Jake was sure that he was saying, "Keep me."

"See? He wants to stay with us. He just said so," insisted Jake. Kate shook her head and started toward home again. The little white dog followed right behind them all the way home.

Their mother came out of the house to greet them. Before she could say anything, the little white dog stopped in front of her and started to lick her toes. He looked up at her with his big blue eyes.

"Can we keep him, Mom? Oh, please?" asked Jake.

"He must belong to someone, Jake. It would not be fair to his owners. They would miss him."

Kate had been thinking all the way home. She had an idea. "What if we call the animal shelter and make posters about the lost dog that we found? Then if nobody calls, we can keep him. What do you say, Mom?"

The little white dog just kept licking Mother's toes. Finally, she smiled and answered, "It looks like it's three against one. This little mop sure wants to stay."

Jake and Kate started working on the posters. They put them up on every corner between school and home. They waited to see if anyone would call. No one called on the first day. No one called on the second day. On the third day, a girl called to ask them if they had found her dog, Penny.

"She's a little white dog with long hair and short, stubby legs. She looks like a little mop sweeping the ground." Jake felt like he might cry. He really had wanted to keep the dog. "One more thing," said the voice on the phone. "She has a little round brown spot on the top of her head between her ears. That's why her name is Penny." Now Jake was so happy that he could hardly speak. There was no brown spot on his dog's head.

"I'm sorry," he told the girl. "This is not Penny."

The next several days passed slowly for Kate and Jake, but no one else called about the dog. After two weeks, their mother told them they could keep the little white dog. They named him Blizzard.

1. At the beginning of the story, where were Kate and Jake going?

   a. to school
   b. to a dog show
   c. home from school
   d. to the park

2. Which character in the story first asks Mother for the dog?

   a. Kate
   b. Jake
   c. Penny
   d. the telephone caller

3. Why did Mother not want to keep the dog?

   a. It could not do any tricks.
   b. It was dirty.
   c. It might already belong to someone else.
   d. It was too little.

4. Who thinks of a plan to try to keep the dog?

   a. Kate
   b. Jake
   c. Mother
   d. the telephone caller

5. Who was Penny?

   a. a neighbor
   b. Jake's new dog
   c. the telephone caller's dog
   d. none of the above

6. How did Jake feel when he first heard the caller describe her lost dog as a mop?

   a. Jake felt sorry for the dog.
   b. Jake was mad at Penny.
   c. Jake felt sad.
   d. none of the above

7. How did Jake feel at the end of the phone call?

   a. confused
   b. mad
   c. sad
   d. none of the above

8. What did they name the little white dog?

   a. Mop
   b. Little White Dog
   c. Penny
   d. Blizzard

9. How were Penny and Blizzard different?

   a. Blizzard had a brown spot on her head, but Penny did not.
   b. One was black and one was white.
   c. One was larger than the other.
   d. Penny had a brown spot on her head, but Blizzard did not.

10. Which of the following statements is true?

   a. Kate and Jake wanted to keep the dog.
   b. Kate did not want to keep the dog.
   c. Father did not want to keep the dog.
   d. Penny wanted to stay with Blizzard.

11. How did Kate change in the story?

    a. At first, she tried to talk Jake out of keeping the dog, and then she tried to talk Mother out of keeping the dog.

    b. At first, she was afraid of the dog, but then she became more afraid.

    c. At first she tried to hide the dog from her mother, and then she told the truth.

    d. At first, she tried to talk Jake out of keeping the dog, and then she tried to help him keep the dog.

12. When Mother said, "It looks like it's three against one," what did she mean?

    a. She thought that the little dog did not want to stay.

    b. She knew that the girl would call on the telephone.

    c. She knew that Penny was missing.

    d. She thought that Kate, Jake, and the little white dog wanted to be together.

13. When Jake first asked Mother if the dog could stay with them, what did she think?

    a. She thought that the dog must belong to someone else and have another home.

    b. She thought that the dog had never had a home.

    c. She thought that the dog did not want to stay with Kate and Jake.

    d. She thought he needed to be cleaned with a mop.

14. In the middle of the story,

    a. A little white dog follows Jake and Kate home from school.

    b. Kate does not want to keep the dog.

    c. Kate and Jake make posters about the lost dog and wait to see if his owner will call.

    d. Kate and Jake name the dog.

15. In the story's ending,

    a. A little white dog follows Jake and Kate home from school.

    b. Kate does not want to keep the dog.

    c. Kate and Jake make posters about the lost dog.

    d. Kate and Jake name the dog.

Practice Skill: WORD ANALYSIS AND
VOCABULARY DEVELOPMENT

Expectation: Use letter sounds, syllables, and word parts to read words.

Tip: A big part of reading is listening to sounds and being able to match a spoken word with a printed word. The exercises in this section will help you with these skills.

Directions for Exercises 1 – 10: Ask a fluent reader to read the directions and words in each of the following exercises. Choose the best answer from the choices on the next pages.

Exercise # 1 – Initial Consonants - Directions: Listen for the beginning sound of the word that I say. On page 35, read across the row and circle the word that has the same beginning sound as the word I say.

1. can	6. mat	11. lost
2. pill	7. new	12. ride
3. bus	8. sun	13. tunnel
4. jet	9. give	14. wish
5. fox	10. hump	15. big

Exercise # 2 - Final Consonants - Directions: Listen for the last sound of the word that I say. On page 36, read across the row and circle the word that has the same ending sound as the word I say.

1. cut	5. toss	9. tub
2. sun	6. food	10. dream
3. fog	7. call	11. fox
4. nap	8. tar	12. kind

Exercise # 3 - Short Vowels - Directions: Listen for the vowel sound in the middle of the word that I say. On page 37, read across the row and circle the word that has the same vowel sound as the word that I say.

1. cup	5. glad	9. pan
2. fill	6. mud	10. set
3. glass	7. get	11. give
4. block	8. six	12. clod

Exercise # 4 - Long Vowels - Directions: Listen for the vowel sound in the middle of the word that I say. On page 38, read across the row and circle the word that has the same vowel sound as the word that I say.

1. toad
2. same
3. pint
4. mule

5. gripe
6. made
7. tote
8. fake

9. freed
10. time
11. oats
12. steam

Exercise # 5 - Initial Digraphs - Directions: Listen for the first sound in the word that I say. On page 39, read across the row and circle the word that begins with the same sound as the word that I say.

1. shudder
2. thimble
3. whistle

4. chimney
5. short
6. thought

7. china
8. shiver
9. whale

Exercise # 6 - Final Digraphs - Directions: Listen for the last sound in the word that I say. On page 40, read across the row and circle the word that ends with the same sound as the word that I say.

1. push
2. cloth
3. each

4. fish
5. rich
6. north

7. catch
8. wash
9. fourth

Exercise # 7　　Initial Blends - Directions: Listen for the consonant blend in the beginning of the word that I say. On page 41, read across the row and circle the word that begins with the same consonant blend as the word that I say.

1. black
2. crib
3. great
4. brush
5. clear

6. drop
7. flag
8. frost
9. glass
10. plant

11. slide
12. pretty
13. stuck
14. snack
15. smart

Exercise # 8 - Final Blends - Directions: Listen for the consonant blend at the end of the word that I say. On page 42, read across the row and circle the word that ends with the same consonant blend as the word that I say.

1. wasp
2. last
3. wand

4. grant
5. crust
6. crisp

7. pond
8. font
9. grand

Exercise # 9 - Rhyming Words - Directions: Listen to the word I say. On pages 43-44, read across the row and circle the word in the list that rhymes with the word that I say.

1.   crab
2.   shape
3.   land
4.   had
5.   space
6.   snail
7.   paid
8.   quack
9.   hair
10. shade
11. flag
12. page

13. track
14. cap
15. star
16. shake
17. tame
18. cane
19. men
20. snail
21. neat
22. cash
23. dear
24. state

25. fine
26. pat
27. win
28. kick
29. trip
30. pill
31. told
32. five
33. bump
34. boat

Exercise # 10 - Rhyming Words Directions: Listen to the clues that I say. On page 45, read across the row and choose the word that best answers the question.

1.   It's the place where you show your smile, and it rhymes with space.

2.   It's where the train travels, and it rhymes with back.

3.   The post office delivers it to your house, and it rhymes with pail.

4.   It's a fruit to eat in the summer, and it rhymes with reach.

5.   We do it with our noses, and it rhymes with fell.

6.   It's making music with your voice, and it rhymes with king.

7.   It's what you dig with a shovel, and it rhymes with pole.

8.   It's a sign that there's a fire, and it rhymes with joke.

9.   It's a valuable metal that we wear as jewelry, and it rhymes with mold.

10. It gives us a way to move water, and it rhymes with chose.

11. It's an insect that usually crawls, and it rhymes with hug.

12. It's where your trash goes, and it rhymes with jump.

Exercise # 1 – Listen to the word. Read across the row and circle the word that has the same beginning sound as the word that you hear.

1.　cool　　　　pan　　　　fat　　　　map

2.　fill　　　　apple　　　　pan　　　　by

3.　sub　　　　bad　　　　grab　　　　dig

4.　large　　　　put　　　　jacks　　　　get

5.　fool　　　　box　　　　off　　　　pick

6.　mule　　　　time　　　　pat　　　　top

7.　win　　　　knock　　　　mop　　　　he

8.　sip　　　　fun　　　　pass　　　　nut

9.　can　　　　love　　　　gone　　　　slap

10.　ham　　　　map　　　　vase　　　　net

11.　train　　　　love　　　　cry　　　　sip

12.　run　　　　dip　　　　cost　　　　trust

13.　time　　　　lost　　　　kill　　　　dirt

14.　shine　　　　now　　　　will　　　　school

15.　ball　　　　gum　　　　pig　　　　duck

Exercise # 2 – Listen to the word. Read across the row and circle the word that has the same ending sound as the word that you hear.

1.   cool   pan   fat   map

2.   pan   rat   tip   nap

3.   fun   grab   tag   goof

4.   prune   soap   cat   call

5.   tap   bus   still   split

6.   add   fan   spoon   rule

7.   with   will   like   pat

8.   ton   dear   trip   part

9.   back   truck   still   job

10.   drive   from   meal   feed

11.   fix   clock   crush   last

12.   found   keep   nice   neat

Exercise # 3 – Listen to the word. Read across the row and circle the word that has the same vowel sound as the word that you hear.

1. cool   run   fat   mop

2. wish   man   head   cash

3. wash   tap   put   if

4. tip   tap   wet   top

5. dog   park   that   glue

6. pup   mad   mop   pen

7. was   put   good   went

8. pick   socks   get   tap

9. pane   sat   no   pen

10. sit   sat   then   up

11. him   got   get   good

12. clap   clock   clue   cluck

Exercise # 4 – Listen to the word. Read across the row and circle the word that has the same vowel sound as the word that you hear.

1. loaf   top   lost   room

2. get   some   gave   soon

3. put   kite   pit   cat

4. up   tune   mill   told

5. pick   good   pool   ice

6. tape   tap   head   did

7. tell   poke   lip   tail

8. fat   mop   took   mail

9. leaf   pet   fun   dog

10. tip   like   tag   top

11. top   fun   road   cook

12. big   sea   stand   so

Exercise # 5 – Listen to the word. Read across the row and circle the word that has the same beginning sound as the word that you hear.

1.	shame	fish	fine	some
2.	fast	think	tree	with
3.	write	white	yellow	under
4.	rich	inch	can	chase
5.	sort	wash	she	sleep
6.	bath	thank	top	time
7.	chest	clap	lunch	just
8.	shop	push	silver	choose
9.	which	you	push	ship

Exercise # 6 – Listen to the word. Read across the row and circle the word that has the same ending sound as the word that you hear.

1.   she   wish   pass   of

2.   this   off   both   kiss

3.   chop   fish   pick   much

4.   pass   shall   wash   with

5.   such   fix   pick   mit

6.   fort   path   this   word

7.   inch   chair   fast   chip

8.   shirt   teach   dish   fix

9.   there   teeth   off   love

Exercise # 7 – Listen to the word. Read across the row and circle the word that has the same beginning sound (consonant blend) as the word that you hear.

1.   boy   brick   blow   table

2.   came   cry   pack   inch

3.   good   cry   grow   train

4.   bring   book   rush   shoe

5.   color   class   quick   there

6.   trim   done   did   dream

7.   flower   fish   three   free

8.   fresh   fall   flea   three

9.   pass   gas   grass   glad

10.   land   play   print   pile

11.   sweater   silly   sleep   spit

12.   prize   play   put   pick

13.   sick   still   slide   sport

14.   sock   smoke   snap   stop

15.   stop   snake   small   slow

Exercise # 8 – Listen to the word. Read across the row and circle the word that has the same ending sound (consonant blend) as the word that you hear.

1. spot   wish   crisp   fast

2. fist   stream   let   pack

3. odd   find   last   crime

4. grow   past   ring   pant

5. crib   fist   bus   brush

6. ask   gasp   split   spend

7. end   hid   front   gone

8. when   spent   friend   fun

9. great   ant   spend   pen

Exercise # 9 – Listen to the word. Read across the row and circle the word that rhymes with the word that you hear.

1.	mad	tab	crust	bat
2.	shade	map	tape	show
3.	stand	load	stay	slag
4.	pan	past	hand	glad
5.	face	smile	pant	part
6.	snow	mail	snap	tape
7.	pad	back	afraid	rid
8.	quit	creek	cake	pack
9.	car	push	stair	hat
10.	fade	shame	fad	mate
11.	drag	glide	flip	float
12.	pat	stage	step	pad
13.	snack	train	trip	take
14.	cape	mope	cat	trap
15.	stand	car	stick	can
16.	stand	shack	cake	cat

17.	name	tap	time	lamp
18.	can	plane	stay	cry
19.	mean	plain	then	fine
20.	fool	snap	roll	mail
21.	nest	net	treat	green
22.	smash	shine	smile	snow
23.	deed	stone	step	clear
24.	date	stack	pat	pit
25.	ship	shine	fire	fry
26.	brat	pit	pine	fate
27.	with	grin	pine	want
28.	pine	cone	thick	kite
29.	tribe	try	pit	grip
30.	plan	lap	drill	pile
31.	top	fold	dip	dust
32.	drive	fast	find	off
33.	stool	add	come	stump
34.	blast	book	float	bat

Exercise # 10 – Listen to the clues. Read across the row and circle the word that answers the question.

1. car   face   pass   bat

2. take   meat   tape   track

3. main   stand   mail   letter

4. peach   apple   berry   glad

5. sniff   smell   bell   smart

6. song   say   sing   hum

7. dirt   tool   stick   hole

8. hot   smoke   stove   pack

9. gold   tin   step   penny

10. fade   lake   hose   tap

11. truck   bug   worm   feet

12. can   box   sink   dump

Exercise # 11 - Read the given word. Emphasize the underlined sound. Then read the choices to find another word that has the same <u>sound</u> as the underlined part.

1. c<u>ar</u>

    a. fair
    b. can
    c. ran
    d. star

2. st<u>ai</u>n

    a. head
    b. man
    c. mane
    d. stew

3. <u>s</u>ave

    a. fish
    b. face
    c. those
    d. wise

4. <u>z</u>ipper

    a. was
    b. side
    c. us
    d. person

5. li<u>v</u>e

    a. life
    b. off
    c. of
    d. loaf

Tip: Good readers often read words by "sounding out" each letter or chunks of letters in the words. They also spot small words within larger words. The exercises below will help you practice these skills.

Exercise # 12 - Which small word or word chunk is <u>not</u> part of the given word?

1. yesterday

    a. yes
    b. day
    c. er
    d. man

2. understand

    a. under
    b. stand
    c. un
    d. some

3. factory

    a. tion
    b. tor
    c. fact
    d. or

4. lemonade

    a. late
    b. lemon
    c. ade
    d. on

5. fisherman

    a. show
    b. man
    c. fish
    d. fisher

Exercise # 13 – Sight Words – Choose the word that best completes the sentence.

1. Can _____ please hand me my coat?

      a. dog
      b. hand
      c. you
      d. said

2. I do not _____ any pets.

      a. go
      b. stripe
      c. bread
      d. have

3. Sunday is the last day _____ the week.

      a. because
      b. of
      c. sweater
      d. do

4. When will Tom _____ home from camp?

      a. want
      b. come
      c. came
      d. does

5. Someday I _____ like to star in a play.

      a. would
      b. guess
      c. act
      d. love

6. The summer breeze came _____ the window.

       a. special
       b. three
       c. through
       d. there

7. My mom likes to _____ me lots of hugs.

       a. give
       b. great
       c. grow
       d. ground

8. I never _____ that I did the job.

       a. want
       b. start
       c. should
       d. said

9. Tess _____ win every race this year

       a. want
       b. could
       c. colors
       d. coming

10. Many _____ ride on the bus to go to the fair.

       a. purple
       b. planet
       c. people
       d. planned

11. Man cannot _____ without food and water.

       a. liver
       b. lost
       c. live
       d. life

12. I think I know _____ will win the contest.

       a. whose
       b. hose
       c. who
       d. why

13. What _____ Myra think of your new haircut?

       a. dish
       b. does
       c. drag
       d. doll

14. I eat a banana every day _____ it is good for me.

       a. because
       b. better
       c. beast
       d. beautiful

15. _____ can I go to buy some flowers?

       a. Whisper
       b. Where
       c. Wash
       d. Wonder

16. Mora has a _____ smile.

       a. bunches
       b. battle
       c. beautiful
       d. butter

17. What is your _____ flavor of ice cream?

       a. flatest
       b. foolish
       c. fantastic
       d. favorite

Exercise # 14 - Read the sentence. Focus on the word that has some sounds underlined. Circle the word that has the same sounds as the underlined letters.

1. I enjoy choosing a b<u>oo</u>k at the library.

      a. choose
      b. shoe
      c. cookie
      d. zoo

2. My dad s<u>ai</u>d that he was proud of me.

      a. red
      b. free
      c. pray
      d. flat

3. It is not r<u>igh</u>t to tease a friend.

      a. fill
      b. bought
      c. bring
      d. pile

4. I w<u>oul</u>d like to try riding a horse some day.

      a. good
      b. out
      c. proud
      d. told

5. Anya's joke made me l<u>augh</u>.

      a. lunch
      b. staff
      c. log
      d. luck

Exercise # 15 Compound Words – Read each sentence. Then choose the word that goes with the underlined word to make a compound word. Make sure that the new word makes sense in the sentence.

1. We will save gas if we _____ <u>pool</u>.

      a. swimming
      b. car
      c. watch
      d. foot

2. Saul is so tall that it is hard to <u>over</u>_____ him.

      a. try
      b. sell
      c. look
      d. tooth

3. I enjoy riding my bicycle every <u>week</u>_____.

      a. month
      b. man
      c. end
      d. land

4. I tried to turn the _____ <u>knob</u>.

      a. glass
      b. wind
      c. out
      d. door

5. Don't forget to tie your _____ <u>lace</u>.

      a. shoe
      b. hand
      c. watch
      d. pin

Read the words. Circle the compound word in each list.

6.   a. handcuff
          b. surprise
          c. suffer
          d. sandwich

7.   a. peaceful
          b. fireplace
          c. flying
          d. repeat

8.   a. sweet potato
          b. wallet
          c. driveway
          d. sister

9.   a. repeat
          b. smelly
          c. before
          d. flashlight

10.   a. lightning
          b. super
          c. selfish
          d. backyard

11.   a. sunny
          b. freedom
          c. homemade
          d. finally

12.   a. weekly
          b. newspaper
          c. person
          d. napkin

13.   a. notebook
          b. hungry
          c. western
          d. foolish

Exercise # 16 - Categories - Read the words in each exercise. Choose the category that best describes the words.

1.　　train　　　airplane　　　　car　　　　　bus

    a. ways to travel
    b. places to shop
    c. things to eat
    d. ways to fly

2.　　doll　　　jump rope　　　ball　　　　jacks

    a. things to jump on
    b. things to bounce
    c. things to eat
    d. things to play with

3.　　lion　　　eagle　　　alligator　　　turkey

    a. pets
    b. wild animals
    c. farm animals
    d. animals with four legs

4.　　orange　　banana　　　grape　　　apple

    a. colors
    b. fruits
    c. vegetables
    d. things to wear

5.　　book　　　letter　　　email　　　magazine

    a. poems
    b. photographs
    c. things to read
    d. things to take to the movies

6.　　boots　　　sandals　　　tennis shoes　　slippers

    a. things to wear on a hike
    b. things to wear on your feet
    c. things to wear on your head
    d. things to wear to bed

Read the category. Then choose the word that does <u>not</u> belong in the given category.

7. hats

    a. cap
    b. socks
    c. baseball cap
    d. cowboy hat

8. furniture

    a. window
    b. chair
    c. table
    d. desk

9. safety gear

    a. helmet
    b. knee pads
    c. gloves
    d. band aid

10. farm animals

    a. pig
    b. sheep
    c. cow
    d. wolf

11. parts of a car

    a. wheel
    b. snow
    c. tire
    d. door

Practice Skill: CONTRACTIONS

Expectation: Identify and make contractions.

Tip: A contraction is two words joined together with one or more letters dropped and replaced by an apostrophe ('). (Do not = don't, I will = I'll). If you are having trouble with contractions, try using them in a sentence. For example, say to yourself, "I will not be afraid." Then think of another way to say the same thing using a contraction: "I won't be afraid." It works! The contraction for "will not" is "won't."

Exercise # 1 - Read the sentence. Choose the contraction for the underlined words.

1.   I <u>do not</u> want to go to camp.

        a.   doesn't
        b.   can't
        c.   wasn't
        d.   don't

2.   She <u>does not</u> understand the story.

        a.   don't
        b.   doesn't
        c.   won't
        d.   wouldn't

3.   You <u>are not</u> trying your best.

        a.   aren't
        b.   won't
        c.   can't
        d.   don't

4.   My mother <u>would not</u> let me go swimming.

        a.   won't
        b.   couldn't
        c.   wouldn't
        d.   shouldn't

5.   Underline the contraction in each sentence below.

   a. We wanted him to come over, but he can't.

   b. She doesn't understand why her friend will not go.

   c. Won't you please help me check my homework?

   d. Isn't that a furry cat?

6.   Draw a line to match each pair of words with its contraction.

   a. we could not   they wouldn't

   b. I should not   she'd

   c. they would not   I'd

   d. you would not   you wouldn't

   e. he would not   we couldn't

   f. I would   she wouldn't

   g. she would not   I shouldn't

   h. she would   he wouldn't

Exercise # 2 - Choose the correct contraction for each pair of words.

1. we are

    a. were
    b. we'd
    c. we'll
    d. we're

2. will not

    a. willn't
    b. won't
    c. we've
    d. will

3. I would

    a. I'd
    b. I wouldn't
    c. I'll
    d. I'ld

4. does not

a. don't
b. doesn't
c. didn't
d. do'nt

5. do not

    a. don't
    b. doesn't
    c. didn't
    d. do'nt

6. did not

    a. don't
    b. doesn't
    c. didn't
    d. did'nt

Practice Skill: CAPITALIZATION

Expectation: Recognize errors in capitalization.

Tip: Use capital letters to begin a sentence; for proper names of people, for names of particular places and things, and for the pronoun *I*.

Read the sentence. Pay attention to capitalization. If there are no mistakes, select choice "d. No mistakes." If the sentence contains one or more mistakes in capitalization, choose the sentence that corrects all the errors.

1. what do you want to do after school?

    a. What do you want to do after school?
    b. what do You want to do after school?
    c. What do You want to do after school?
    d. No mistakes

2. yes, i want to play outside today.

    a. yes, I want to play outside today.
    b. Yes, i want to play outside today.
    c. Yes, I want to play outside today.
    d. No mistakes

3. susan thinks that i should name my dog pogo.

    a. Susan thinks that I should name my dog pogo.
    b. Susan thinks that i should name my dog Pogo.
    c. Susan thinks that I should name my dog Pogo.
    d. No mistakes

4. Mother's favorite fairy tale character is Cinderella.

    a. mother's favorite fairy tale character is cinderella.
    b. Mother's favorite fairy tale character is cinderella.
    c. mother's favorite fairy tale character is Cinderella.
    d. No mistakes

5. Mrs. james is the name of my teacher.

    a. Mrs. James is the name of my teacher.
    b. mrs. james is the name of my teacher.
    c. Mrs. james is the Name of my Teacher.
    d. no mistakes

6. I think i will read a Book now.

    a. I Think I will Read a Book Now.
    b. I think i will read a book now.
    c. I think I will read a book now.
    d. no mistakes

7. We live near the park.

    a. We live near the Park.
    b. We live near The Park.
    c. We live Near The Park.
    d. no mistakes

8. We live near Old Oak Park.

    a. We live near old oak park.
    b. We live near Old Oak park.
    c. We live near old oak Park
    d. no mistakes

9. Next week uncle joe is coming to visit us.

    a. Next week uncle Joe is coming to visit Us.
    b. Next week Uncle Joe is coming to visit us.
    c. Next Week Uncle joe is coming to visit us.
    d. no mistakes

Practice Skill: PUNCTUATION

Expectation: Correctly use periods, question marks, exclamation points, and commas in sentences.

Tip:
Use a period:
- to end a statement.
- after an abbreviation such as Dr. or Mrs., or St. or Ave.

Use a question mark:
- to end a question.

Use an exclamation point:
- after a word, phrase, or sentence that shows strong feelings.

Use a comma:
- after each word in a series of three or more.
- after a city name if the state follows.
- after a greeting of a letter.
- after the closing of a letter.
- in dates, after the day of the month and before the year.

Read the sentence. Pay attention to punctuation. If there are no mistakes, select choice "d. All are correct." If the sentence contains mistakes in punctuation, choose the sentence that corrects all the errors.

1. Do you want to go to the movies?

   a. Do you want to go to the movies.
   b. Do you want to go to the movies!
   c. Do you want to go to the movies,
   d. No mistakes

2. Yikes. Watch out for the bee?

   a. Yikes. Watch out for the bee.
   b. Yikes? Watch out for the bee?
   c. Yikes! Watch out for the bee!
   d. No mistakes

3.   Help. Help? I'm locked in the bathroom,

   a. Help? Help? I'm locked in the bathroom?
   b. Help! Help! I'm locked in the bathroom,
   c. Help! Help! I'm locked in the bathroom!
   d. No mistakes.

4.   June 30 2001

   a. June, 30, 2001
   b. June, 30 2001,
   c. June 30, 2001
   d. No mistakes.

5.   I live in Montrose, California

   a. I live in Montrose California
   b. I live in, Montrose California.
   c. I live in Montrose, California.
   d. No mistakes.

6.   I ate an apple a sandwich a cookie and carrot sticks for lunch.

   a. I ate an apple a sandwich a cookie, and carrot sticks for lunch.
   b. I ate an, apple, a, sandwich, a, cookie, and, carrot, sticks, for lunch.
   c. I ate an apple, a sandwich, a cookie, and carrot sticks for lunch.
   d. No mistakes.

7.   My dentist's name is Dr. Good.

   a. My dentist's name is Dr. Good?
   b. My dentist's, name, is Dr. Good.
   c. My dentist's name is. Dr. Good.
   d. No mistakes.

8. Have you ever been to the zoo?

   a. Have you ever been to the zoo.
   b. Have you ever been to the zoo,
   c. Have you ever been to the zoo!
   d. No mistakes

Practice Skill: WORD USAGE

Expectation: Use words correctly in sentences.

> Tip: When you do each of these exercises, read the sentence and say "Mmmmm" when you come to the blank. Then read the sentence again, but this time substitute the first word choice for the "Mmmmm." Do this until you have substituted each word choice for the blank in the sentence. Listen to the sound of each sentence. This will help you eliminate many choices.

Try each answer choice in the blank. Choose the word or words that best fit in the sentence.

1. One twin is _____ than the other.
   a. short
   b. shorter
   c. shortest
   d. none of the above

2. I bought a pair of _____ at the store.
   a. socks
   b. sock
   c. sockses
   d. none of the above

3. Ben _____ his books to school.
   a. take
   b. taked
   c. took
   d. none of the above

4. We _____ all our money on toys.
   a. spent
   b. spends
   c. spended
   d. none of the above

5. Mr. Palmer _____ up the stairs.

    a. goed
    b. want
    c. runned
    d. none of the above

6. The flag _____ in the wind.

    a. was blowing
    b. were blowing
    c. blowed
    d. none of the above

7. I _____ understood what he was saying.

    a. will
    b. never
    c. could not
    d. none of the above

8. He _____ in the lake.

    a. swim
    b. swimming
    c. swimmed
    d. none of the above

9. The baby _____ all night long.

    a. cry
    b. cried
    c. crying
    d. none of the above

10. We _____ our dog to the park.

    a. bringed
    b. brung
    c. brought
    d. none of the above

Practice Skills : SENTENCE STRUCTURE AND
CONTENT ORGANIZATION

Expectation: Recognize correct sentence organization
and structure.

Tip: Good writers organize their thoughts and write them down clearly to make it easy for their readers to understand. They think about the what happens first, next, and last. They make a list, an outline, or a map of what they want to write. After they write a first draft, they edit it to make it as clear as it can be.

As you do the following exercises, think about what the writer is trying to say. Edit the sentences to make them clearer.

Exercise # 1 - Read the sentences. Then read the choices to see if one of them expresses the thought in a better way. If none of the choices is better than the original sentence, choose "d. No change."

1. Tom took a walk. Across the street. He walked carefully.

    a. Tom carefully walked. Across the street carefully.
    b. Carefully walked across the street went Tom.
    c. Tom carefully walked across the street.
    d. No change.

2. Looking for the fireworks last year and we got lost that last Fourth of July last year.

    a. That last Fourth of July, we got lost last year. And we got lost last time. The fireworks was what we were looking for last year.
    b. Last year we got lost. Last year we looked for fireworks. Last year we got lost. Last year on Fourth of July.
    c. Last year on the Fourth of July, we got lost while we were looking for fireworks.
    d. No change.

3. We went to the lake, we went swimming, we had a picnic? We had fun.

    a. We went to the lake, and we went swimming, and we had a picnic, and we had fun.

    b. We went to the lake. We went swimming. We had a picnic. We had fun.

    c. We had fun at the lake. We went swimming and had a picnic.

    d. No change.

4. At the zoo, we saw animals from around the world. Tigers my favorite.

    a. We saw animals from around the world and we saw tigers my favorite zoo.

    b. At the zoo, we saw tigers from my favorite world around the zoo. My favorite.

    c. At the zoo, we saw animals from around the world. The tigers were my favorite.

    d. No change.

5. She walked to school, got out of bed, and then she woke up and gave her dad a hug goodbye.

    a. She walked to school. She got out of bed. She woke up. And she gave her dad a goodbye hug.

    b. After she woke up and got out of bed, she gave her dad a goodbye hug, and walked to school.

    c. After she walked to school, she woke up, got out of bed, and gave her dad a goodbye hug.

    d. No change.

Exercise # 2 – Read the choices in each exercise. One of the choices is not a complete sentence. Mark the choice that is <u>not</u> a complete sentence. Do not let the capitalization and punctuation fool you.

1.   a.   I have a dog.
       b.   Named Sandy.
       c.   My dog does tricks for me.
       d.   She likes to play fetch.

2.   a.   Recess time is fun.
       b.   I like to talk and play with my friends.
       c.   Sometimes we play on the swings.
       d.   The bars, too.

3.   a.   What is your favorite food?
       b.   Pizza, fruits, or salad?
       c.   I enjoy peanut butter and jelly sandwiches.
       d.   I do not like yellow cheese on anything.

4.   a.   On vacation.
       b.   I like to stay home and play with my friends.
       c.   What do you like to do?
       d.   Have you ever been on an airplane?

5.   a.   Let's play a game.
       b.   You go first.
       c.   Be careful when you run.
       d.   Any game.

6.   a.   My favorite ice cream flavors are.
       b.   Chocolate chip tastes delicious.
       c.   Would you like a taste?
       d.   That looks yummy.

7.   a.   I like to stay indoors when it rains.
       b.   When it rains.
       c.   I may read a book in bed.
       d.   I might stay in my pajamas all day.

Practice Skills: STUDY SKILLS

Expectation: Use alphabetizing skills to locate information.

Tip: It is important to know how to alphabetize words (put them in A-B-C order) and how to find a particular word in an alphabetized list. Why is this so? Most resource books contain thousands of facts, and they are written so that you do not have to read them from start to finish. Very few people read an entire encyclopedia or dictionary! Because those books are organized in alphabetical order, it is easy to find information in them. Many other books have an index (an alphabetical list of topics that are contained in the book and the pages where you can read about that topic). The exercises in this section will help you apply your alphabetizing skills so that you can be a fast researcher.

Read the question and choose the best answer.

1. Which word comes first in alphabetical order?

    a. made
    b. foot
    c. car
    d. dog

2. Which word comes first in alphabetical order?

    a. Ants
    b. Spiders
    c. Moths
    d. Butterflies

3. Which word comes first in alphabetical order?
    a. why
    b. you
    c. zipper
    d. top

Practice Skills: SPELLING

Expectation: Correctly spell frequently used words and irregular words such as *was, were, says, said, who, what, why.* Correctly spell words with basic short-vowel patterns.

Tip: Many words are spelled exactly the way they sound. There are other words that follow a pattern. The others need to be learned by memorizing the sequence of the letters. As you do these exercises, think about whether the word follows a spelling rule, is spelled like it sounds, or whether it is one that you just have to memorize.

Exercise # 1 - Read the clue. Use it to unscramble each word.

1. This wild animal that looks like a small dog with a bushy tail.

   xof   _____

2. This animal makes a good pet and likes to purr.

   act   _____

3. Players use this to hit a ball.

   tab   _____

4. If you just want a taste of something and not a bite, you might do this.

   cilk   _____

5. The last person in line stands in this place.

   den   _____

6. If there are two of us in a room, one person is me, and this is the other one.

   uyo   _____

Exercise # 2 –   Read the clue. Use it to choose the correct word.

1. When we see this fly, it makes us feel proud.

    a.   golf
    b.   flower
    c.   flag
    d.   flat

2.   This is a good place to take a bath.

    a.   tan
    b.   top
    c.   tub
    d.   tip

3.   If you want to know the time, you look at this.

    a.   click
    b.   clock
    c.   clack
    d.   cluck

4. To pick something up, you would have to do this.

    a. lift
    b. loft
    c. land
    d. luck

5. This goes around your waist to keep your clothes from falling down.

    a. boat
    b. blue
    c. big
    d. belt

6. A pair of scissors can help you do this.

    a.   cat
    b.   cute
    c.   cut
    d.   color

Exercise # 3 – Read each sentence. Look at the underlined word to see which one is spelled the wrong way. Choose the one that is <u>not</u> spelled correctly. If all the words are spelled correctly, choose "d. no mistake."

1. We <u>are</u> in <u>the</u> first grade <u>thiss</u> year .

    a. are   b. the   c. thiss   d. no mistake

2. <u>Wat</u> <u>do</u> <u>you</u> want to do after school?

    a. Wat   b. do   c. you   d. no mistake

3. <u>Wil</u> she <u>tell</u> me about her <u>trip</u>?

    a. Wil   b. tell   c. trip   d. no mistake

4. I do <u>not</u> <u>know</u> his <u>last</u> name.

    a. not   b. know   c. last   d. no mistake

5. My dad <u>wants</u> to buy a <u>noo</u> <u>car</u>.

    a. wants   b. noo   c. car   d. no mistake

6. My aunt <u>lives</u> <u>next</u> to a <u>lak</u>.

    a. lives   b. next   c. lak   d. no mistake

7. <u>Did</u> you hear <u>what</u> she <u>sed</u> to Jack?

    a. Did   b. what   c. sed   d. no mistake

8. <u>When</u> will <u>we</u> <u>eet</u> dinner?

    a. When   b. we   c. eet   d. no mistake

9. She <u>walked</u> <u>home</u> <u>frum</u> the store.

    a. walked   b. home   c. frum   d. no mistake

Exercise # 4 - Read each sentence. Think of a word that makes sense in the blank. Mark the choice that fits the meaning of the sentence and is spelled correctly.

1. I saw a _____ cat.

   a. balk
   b. black
   c. ball
   d. block

2. I _____ a pet.

   a. want
   b. whant
   c. wunt
   d. waunt

3. She _____ a bike to school.

   a. rids
   b. ridz
   c. rides
   d. rieds

4. Will you play _____ me?

   a. whith
   b. wiht
   c. wit
   d. with

5. It is my birthday. I am _____ today.

   a. happy
   b. hapy
   c. heppy
   d. hoppy

ANSWER KEY
LANGUAGE ARTS

Reading
Comprehension

Exercise #1
1. C
2. A
3. D
4. A
5. B
6. C
7. D
8. A
9. C
10. D
11. D
12. B
13. C
14. A
15. B
16. C
17. C
18. D

Exercise # 2
1. C
2. B
3. C
4. B
5. B

Exercise # 3
1. C
2. D
3. C
4. B
5. A
6. D

Exercise # 4
1. C
2. C
3. A
4. C
5. D
6. D
7. D
8. B
9. D
10. A

Exercise # 5
1. B
2. B
3. A
4. C
5. C
6. A
7. D
8. B

Exercise # 6
1. A
2. C
3. D
4. C
5. C

Exercise # 7
1. D
2. C
3. D
4. A
5. B
6. C
7. B
8. D
9. B

Exercise # 8
1. C
2. D
3. C
4. D
5. A
6. B
7. A
8. B

Literary
Response
1. C
2. B
3. C
4. A
5. C
6. C
7. D
8. D

Literary Response
9. D
10. A
11. D
12. D
13. A
14. C
15. D

Word Analysis/
Vocabulary
Development

Exercise # 1
1. cool
2. pan
3. bad
4. jacks
5. fool
6. mule
7. knock
8. sip
9. gone
10. ham
11. love
12. run
13. time
14. will
15. ball

Exercise # 2
1. fat
2. pan
3. tag
4. soap
5. bus
6. add
7. will
8. dear
9. job
10. from
11. fix
12. found

Word Analyis/
Vocabulary

Exercise # 3
1. run
2. wish
3. tap
4. top
5. that
6. pup
7. went
8. pick
9. sat
10. then
11. him
12. clock

Exercise # 4
1. loaf
2. gave
3. kite
4. tune
5. ice
6. tape
7. poke
8. mail
9. leaf
10. like
11. road
12. sea

Exercise #5
1. shame
2. think
3. white
4. chase
5. she
6. thank
7. chest
8. shop
9. which

Exercise # 6
1. wish
2. both
3. much
4. wash
5. such
6. path
7. inch
8. dish

9. teeth

Exercise # 7
1. blow
2. cry
3. grow
4. bring
5. class
6. dream
7. flower
8. fresh
9. glad
10. play
11. sleep
12. prize
13. still
14. snap
15. small

Exercise # 8
1. crisp
2. fist
3. find
4. pant
5. fist
6. gasp
7. end
8. spent
9. spend

Exercise # 9
1. tab
2. tape
3. stand
4. glad
5. face
6. mail
7. afraid
8. pack
9. stair
10. fade
11. drag
12. stage
13. snack
14. trap
15. car
16. cake
17. name
18. plane
19. then

20. mail
21. treat
22. smash
23. clear
24. date
25. shine
26. brat
27. grin
28. thick
29. grip
30. drill
31. fold
32. drive
33. stump
34. float

Exercise # 10
1. face
2. track
3. mail
4. peach
5. smell
6. sing
7. hole
8. smoke
9. gold
10. hose
11. bug
12. dump

Exercise # 11
1. D
2. C
3. B
4. A
5. C

Exercise # 12
1. D
2. D
3. A
4. A
5. A

Word Analysis/
Vocabulary
Exercise # 13
  1. C
  2. D
  3. B
  4. B
  5. A
  6. C
  7. A
  8. D
  9. B
  10. C
  11. C
  12. C
  13. B
  14. A
  15. B
  16. C
  17. D
Exercise # 14
  1. C
  2. A
  3. D
  4. A
  5. B
Exercise # 15
  1. B
  2. C
  3. C
  4. D
  5. A
  6. A
  7. B
  8. C
  9. D
  10. D
  11. C
  12. B
  13. A

Exercise # 16
  1. A
  2. D
  3. B
  4. B
  5. C
  6. B
  7. B
  8. A
  9. D
  10. D
  11. B

Contractions
Exercise # 1
  1. D
  2. B
  3. A
  4. C
  5. a. can't
    b. doesn't
    c. Won't
    d. Isn't
  6. a. we couldn't
    b. I shouldn't
    c. they wouldn't
    d. you wouldn't
    e. he wouldn't
    f. I'd
    g. she wouldn't
    h. she'd
Exercise # 2
  1. D
  2. B
  3. A
  4. B
  5. A
  6. C

Capitalization
  1. A
  2. C
  3. C
  4. D
  5. A
  6. C
  7. D
  8. D
  9. B

Punctuation
  1. D
  2. C
  3. C
  4. C
  5. C
  6. C
  7. D
  8. D

Word Usage
  1. B
  2. A
  3. C
  4. A
  5. D
  6. A
  7. B
  8. D
  9. B
  10. C

Sentence
Structure
Exercise # 1
  1. C
  2. C
  3. C
  4. C
  5. B
Exercise # 2
  1. B
  2. D
  3. B
  4. A
  5. D
  6. A
  7. B

Study Skills
  1. C
  2. A
  3. D

<u>Spelling</u>
Exercise # 1
1. fox
2. cat
3. bat
4. lick
5. end
6. you

Exercise # 2
1. C
2. C
3. B
4. A
5. D
6. C

Exercise # 3
1. C
2. A
3. A
4. D
5. B
6. C
7. C
8. C
9. C

Exercise # 4
1. B
2. A
3. C
4. D
5. A

MATH

Practice Skill: BASIC ADDITION FACTS

Expectation: Solve problems using addition (sums to 20).

> Tip: When you recopy addition problems, be sure to line up the digits so that all the digits in the ones place are directly beneath each other. Use graph paper (paper marked with squares) to help you do this.

Exercise # 1-Solve each problem and choose the correct answer.

1. $6 + 3 =$

   a. 10
   b. 7
   c. 3
   d. 9

2. $4 + 6 =$

   a. 10
   b. 6
   c. 8
   d. 12

3. $5 + 2 =$

   a. 7
   b. 10
   c. 8
   d. 9

4. $2 + 3 =$

   a. 6
   b. 5
   c. 23
   d. 9

5. $3 + 3 =$

   a. 6
   b. 7
   c. 33
   d. 0

6. $5 + 4 =$

   a. 1
   b. 9
   c. 10
   d. 8

7. $7 + 3 =$

   a. 4
   b. 11
   c. 12
   d. 10

8. $5 + 5 =$

   a. 5
   b. 0
   c. 10
   d. 9

Exercise # 2-Solve each problem and choose the correct answer.

1. 9 + 3 =

    a. 10
    b. 6
    c. 23
    d. 12

2. 7 + 9 =

    a. 16
    b. 19
    c. 17
    d. 2

3. 8 + 8 =

    a. 14
    b. 10
    c. 12
    d. 16

4. 8 + 3 =

    a. 10
    b. 5
    c. 12
    d. 11

5. 8 + 7 =

    a. 15
    b. 12
    c. 16
    d. 4

6. 9 + 4 =

    a. 6
    b. 16
    c. 17
    d. 13

7. 7 + 4 =

    a. 3
    b. 11
    c. 10
    d. 12

8. 5 + 9 =

    a. 11
    b. 9
    c. 14
    d. 16

9. 7 + 6 =

    a. 12
    b. 13
    c. 14
    d. 15

10. 7 + 7 =

    a. 15
    b. 0
    c. 14
    d. 19

11. 6 + 9 =

    a. 18
    b. 15
    c. 3
    d. 14

12. 5 + 7 =

    a. 12
    b. 14
    c. 2
    d. 9

Exercise # 3-Solve each problem and choose the correct answer. If the correct answer is not one of the choices, choose "d. not here."

1.   4
       + 3

   a. 1
   b. 6
   c. 7
   d. not here

2.   7
       + 2

   a. 5
   b. 8
   c. 10
   d. not here

3.   6
       + 3

   a. 3
   b. 9
   c. 7
   d. not here

4.   5
       + 0

   a. 5
   b. 6
   c. 0
   d. not here

5.   7 + 1 =

   a. 6
   b. 17
   c. 8
   d. not here

6.   1
       + 9

   a. 8
   b. 10
   c. 0
   d. not here

7.   4
       + 6

   a. 10
   b. 9
   c. 2
   d. not here

8.   3
       + 3

   a. 3
   b. 0
   c. 9
   d. not here

9.   8
       + 2

   a. 6
   b. 4
   c. 10
   d. not here

10.   4 + 5 =

   a. 10
   b. 9
   c. 1
   d. not here

Exercise # 4-Solve each problem and choose the correct answer. If the correct answer is not one of the choices, choose "d. not here."

1.   9
        + 3

    a. 12
    b. 6
    c. 7
    d. not here

2.   7
        + 6

    a. 14
    b. 13
    c. 1
    d. not here

3.   6
        + 5

    a. 13
    b. 12
    c. 11
    d. not here

4.   2
        + 9

    a. 5
    b. 7
    c. 10
    d. not here

5.   10 + 1 =

    a. 11
    b. 9
    c. 101
    d. not here

6.   8
        + 9

    a. 1
    b. 10
    c. 18
    d. not here

7.   4
        + 8

    a. 10
    b. 14
    c. 4
    d. not here

8.   6
        + 6

    a. 12
    b. 0
    c. 9
    d. not here

9.   7
        + 5

    a. 16
    b. 2
    c. 12
    d. not here

10.   6 + 5 =

    a. 10
    b. 1
    c. 11
    d. not here

Practice Skill: BASIC SUBTRACTION FACTS

Expectation: Solve problems using subtraction (corresponding to addition sums to 20).

Tip: Remember that subtraction problems show taking away, comparing, or finding the difference between two amounts.

Exercise # 1-Solve each problem and choose the correct answer. If the correct answer is not one of the choices, choose "d. not here."

1.   6 – 3 =

    a. 9
    b. 6
    c. 3
    d. not here

2.   10 – 4=

    a. 10
    b. 6
    c. 8
    d. not here

3.   7 – 2 =

    a. 5
    b. 9
    c. 3
    d. not here

4.   5 – 3 =

    a. 6
    b. 8
    c. 2
    d. not here

5.   3 – 3 =

    a. 6
    b. 3
    c. 0
    d. not here

6.   9 –5 =

    a. 1
    b. 5
    c. 4
    d. not here

7.   10 – 7=

    a. 17
    b. 1
    c. 2
    d. not here

8.   10 –5 =

    a. 5
    b. 0
    c. 15
    d. not here

Exercise # 2-Solve each problem and choose the correct answer. If the correct answer is not one of the choices, choose "d. not here."

1. $17 - 9 =$

    a. 12
    b. 9
    c. 8
    d. not here

2. $15 - 7 =$

    a. 8
    b. 7
    c. 9
    d. not here

3. $11 - 2 =$

    a. 4
    b. 7
    c. 13
    d. not here

4. $13 - 8 =$

    a. 6
    b. 5
    c. 4
    d. not here

5. $14 - 7 =$

    a. 7
    b. 5
    c. 6
    d. not here

6. $16 - 8 =$

    a. 7
    b. 9
    c. 8
    d. not here

7. $18 - 9 =$

    a. 9
    b. 8
    c. 10
    d. not here

8. $12 - 6 =$

    a. 8
    b. 6
    c. 18
    d. not here

9. $10 - 5 =$

    a. 6
    b. 4
    c. 15
    d. not here

10. $8 - 4 =$

    a. 5
    b. 4
    c. 12
    d. not here

Exercise # 3-Solve each problem and choose the correct answer. If the correct answer is not one of the choices, choose "d. not here."

1.   9
      − 3

   a. 12
   b. 6
   c. 7
   d. not here

2.   10
      − 6

   a. 16
   b. 3
   c. 4
   d. not here

3.   6
      − 4

   a. 10
   b. 2
   c. 1
   d. not here

4.   5
      − 3

   a. 3
   b. 8
   c. 1
   d. not here

5.   10 − 1 =

   a. 11
   b. 9
   c. 101
   d. not here

6.   10
      − 9

   a. 11
   b. 10
   c. 1
   d. not here

7.   9
      − 8

   a. 17
   b. 6
   c. 1
   d. not here

8.   6
      − 6

   a. 12
   b. 0
   c. 9
   d. not here

9.   7
      − 5

   a. 3
   b. 2
   c. 12
   d. not here

10.   9 − 6 =

   a. 9
   b. 2
   c. 3
   d. not here

Exercise # 4-Solve each problem and choose the correct answer. If the correct answer is not one of the choices, choose "d. not here."

1.　　12
　　　 − 3

   a. 15
   b. 6
   c. 7
   d. not here

2.　　14
　　　 − 6

   a. 16
   b. 8
   c. 4
   d. not here

3.　　16
　　　 − 8

   a. 10
   b. 2
   c. 8
   d. not here

4.　　13
　　　 − 7

   a. 14
   b. 8
   c. 4
   d. not here

5.　　14 − 7 =

   a. 13
   b. 7
   c. 11
   d. not here

6.　　18
　　　 − 9

   a. 11
   b. 10
   c. 1
   d. not here

7.　　17
　　　 − 8

   a. 7
   b. 11
   c. 9
   d. not here

8.　　15
　　　 − 7

   a. 12
   b. 0
   c. 9
   d. not here

9.　　16
　　　 − 9

   a. 3
   b. 7
   c. 13
   d. not here

10.　　12 − 6 =

   a. 6
   b. 2
   c. 13
   d. not here

Practice Skill: NUMBER SENSE

Expectation: Understand and use numbers up to 100.

Tip: Think about how one number relates to another number.
Learn the symbols that explain this, such as =, >, < .
> greater than (6 > 2 means 6 is greater than 2)
< less than (3 < 9 means 3 is less than 9)
If you get confused, think of the sign as a mouth that is opening
to take a bite. The mouth is opening to take a big bite and
swallow the "bigger" or greater number. The open mouth faces
the greater number.

**Exercise # 1 - Solve each problem and choose the correct answer. If the
correct answer is not one of the choices, choose "d. not here."**

1.

How many stars are there?

a. 7
b. 5
c. 6
d. not here

2.

How many hearts are there?

a. 30
b. 22
c. 15
d. not here

3.   What number is missing?   7, 8, 9, ☐ , 11

    a. 6
    b. 12
    c. 9
    d. not here

4.   What number is missing?   13, 14, ☐ , 16, 17

    a. 12
    b. 15
    c. 16
    d. not here

5.   Shanna has 7 shells. She finds 4 more. How many does she have all together?

    a. 11 shells
    b. 8 shells
    c. 3 shells
    d. not here

6.   Nina had 12 baseball cards. She gave 3 cards to her best friend. How many cards does she have now?

    a. 12 cards
    b. 15 cards
    c. 9 cards
    d. not here

7.   What is 3 more than 15?

    a. 12
    b. 18
    c. 17
    d. not here

8.   What is 2 less than 14?

    a. 16
    b. 20
    c. 10
    d. not here

9.　　Mr. Brown has 12 cows grazing in the field. There are 4 cows back in the barn giving milk. How many cows does Mr. Brown own?

　　a. 12 cows
　　b. 8 cows
　　c. 16 cows
　　d. not here

10.　　Joel has 3 fish in the family's fish tank. Carolina has 2 more fish than Joel in the tank. How many fish does Carolina have?

　　a. 5 fish
　　b. 2 fish
　　c. 1 fish
　　d. not here

11.　　In exercise 10, how many fish are in the tank in all?

　　　　a. 3 fish
　　　　b. 5 fish
　　　　c. 8 fish
　　　　d. not here

12.　　Mr. Jackson made 10 sandwiches for the Cub Scout meeting. The scouts ate 6 of them. How many sandwiches did the scouts leave?

　　　　a. 16 sandwiches
　　　　b. 6 sandwiches
　　　　c. 4 sandwiches
　　　　d. not here

13.　　Mr. Jackson made 10 sandwiches for the Daisy Scout meeting. There were 2 sandwiches left at the end of their meeting. How many sandwiches did they eat?

　　　　a. 12 sandwiches
　　　　b. 8 sandwiches
　　　　c. 6 sandwiches
　　　　d. not here

What symbol makes the sentence true? Choose your answer from:

a.   <
b.   >
c.   =

14.   6 ◯ 4

15.   3 ◯ 5

16.   5 ◯ 6 – 1

17.   25 ◯ 35

18.   4 + 2 ◯ 2 + 4

19.   6 – 0 ◯ 6 – 3

20.   7 – 3 ◯ 7 – 0

21.   8 – 1 ◯ 8 – 5

22.   9 – 7 ◯ 9 – 2

23.   8 + 2 ◯ 7 + 2

24.   9 + 3 ◯ 9 – 5

25.   7 + 9 ◯ 9 – 7

What symbol makes the sentence true? Choose from: a. +

                                                                b. −

26.   14 $\bigcirc$ 7 = 7

27.   7 $\bigcirc$ 2 = 9

28.   8 $\bigcirc$ 3 = 11

29.   25 $\bigcirc$ 5 = 20

30.   32 $\bigcirc$ 16 = 16

31.   19 $\bigcirc$ 9 = 10

32.   10 $\bigcirc$ 9 = 19

33.   3 $\bigcirc$ 33 = 36

34.   36 $\bigcirc$ 3 = 33

35.   10 $\bigcirc$ 1 = 11

36.   1 $\bigcirc$ 11 = 12

37.   12 $\bigcirc$ 1 = 11

38.   12 $\bigcirc$ 11 = 1

Exercise # 2 – Choose the number that makes the sentence true. If the correct answer is not one of the choices, choose "d. not here."

1.   7 + ☐ = 13

    a. 6
    b. 7
    c. 20
    d. not here

2.   ☐ – 3 = 6

    a. 6
    b. 3
    c. 9
    d. not here

3.   20 – ☐ = 10

    a. 9
    b. 30
    c. 20
    d. not here

4.   ☐ – 8 = 3

    a. 8
    b. 11
    c. 5
    d. not here

5.   23 + ☐ = 33

    a. 10
    b. 11
    c. 13
    d. not here

Tip: When you recopy these problems, be sure to line up the digits so that all the digits in the ones place are directly beneath each other.

Exercise # 3 -   Solve each problem and choose the correct answer. If the correct answer is not one of the choices, choose "d. not here."

1.   5 + 6 + 2 =

    a. 13
    b. 11
    c. 112
    d. not here

2.   4 + 6 + 5 =

    a. 16
    b. 15
    c. 465
    d. not here

3.   2 + 8 + 8 =

    a. 32
    b. 16
    c. 108
    d. not here

4.   4 + 4 + 4 =

    a. 12
    b. 14
    c. 444
    d. not here

5.   24 + 5 =

    a. 74
    b. 47
    c. 29
    d. not here

Exercise # 4 - Which number goes in the box to complete the series?
If the correct answer is not one of the choices, choose "d. not here."

1.   2, ☐ , 6, 8, 10, 12

    a. 3
    b. 4
    c. 5
    d. not here

2.   32, 34, 36, 38, ☐ , 42

    a. 39
    b. 40
    c. 41
    d. not here

3.   5, 10, 15, 20, ☐ , 30

    a. 22
    b. 25
    c. 40
    d. not here

4.   40, 50, ☐ , 70, 80

    a. 55
    b. 65
    c. 60
    d. not here

5.   75, 80, 85, 90, 95, ☐

    a. 90
    b. 100
    c. 105
    d. not here

**Exercise # 5 – Solve each problem and choose the correct answer.
If the correct answer is not one of the choices, choose "d. not here."**

1.　　What coins are shown here?

　　a. 1 quarter, 2 dimes, 1 nickel, 1 penny
　　b. 1 half-dollar, 1 quarter, 3 pennies
　　c. 1 quarter, 1 dime, 2 nickels, 1 penny
　　d. not here

2.　　What coins are shown here?

　　a.　　1 quarter, 2 nickels, 3 dimes
　　b.　　1 nickel, 2 dimes, 3 pennies
　　c.　　1 dime, 2 nickels 3 pennies
　　d.　　not here

3.　　What is the value of 1 quarter and 1 dime?

　　a.　　25 cents
　　b.　　50 cents
　　c.　　35 cents
　　d.　　not here

4.　　What is the value of 2 dimes and 2 nickels?

　　a.　　30 cents
　　b.　　25 cents
　　c.　　35 cents
　　d.　　not here

5. Which coins do <u>not</u> add up to 15 cents?

    a. 1 quarter
    b. 3 nickels
    c. 15 pennies
    d. 1 dime and 1 nickel

6. Which coins add up to 25 cents?

    a. 3 nickels
    b. 2 dimes
    c. 5 nickels
    d. 3 dimes

7. Which coins are worth the same amount?

    a. 5 pennies and 1 dime
    b. 5 pennies and 1 nickel
    c. 5 pennies and 1 quarter
    d. not here

8. Which coins are worth the same amount?

    a. 2 dimes and 1 quarter
    b. 1 quarter and 3 nickels
    c. 1 dime and 2 nickels
    d. not here

9. Which coins are <u>not</u> worth 35 cents?

    a. 3 dimes and 1 nickel
    b. 1 quarter and 1 dime
    c. 2 quarters
    d. 2 dimes and 3 nickels

10. Which coins are <u>not</u> worth 50 cents?

    a. 3 quarters
    b. 5 dimes
    c. 10 nickels
    d. 50 pennies

Practice Skills: ALGEBRA AND FUNCTIONS

Expectation: Write and solve number sentences expressed in problem situations. Recognize possible problem situations that are represented in number sentences.

Tip: The exercises in this section will help you understand the ideas behind the signs and numerals that you work with in math every day.

Choose the best answer to each question. If there is no correct answer, choose "d. not here."

1. Simon is four years younger than Jack. Jack is 9 years old. Which number sentence will tell you Simon's age?

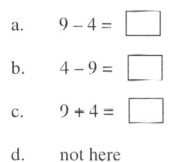

    a. $9 - 4 = \boxed{}$

    b. $4 - 9 = \boxed{}$

    c. $9 + 4 = \boxed{}$

    d.   not here

2. When Chan went swimming, four more children jumped in the pool. Which number sentence shows how many children were in the pool at the same time?

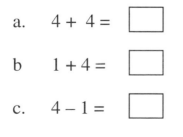

    a. $4 + 4 = \boxed{}$

    b $1 + 4 = \boxed{}$

    c. $4 - 1 = \boxed{}$

    d.   not here

3. Lon is thinking of a number that is five more than 21. What number sentence shows Lon's number?

    a. $21 - 5 =$ ☐

    b. $5 - 21 =$ ☐

    c. $21 + 5 =$ ☐

    d. not here

4. Sonya had 11 candles on her birthday cake. After one blow, 7 candles were still burning. What number sentence shows how many candles Sonya blew out?

    a. $11 + 7 =$ ☐

    b. $11 + 4 =$ ☐

    c. $11 - 7 =$ ☐

    d. not here

5. Which is another way of showing 10?

    a. $12 - 4$
    b. $8 + 2$
    c. $7 + 1 + 3$
    d. not here

6. Chung has 4 pencils. Nina has 2 more pencils than Chung. Tom has 3 more pencils that Nina. How many pencils does Tom have?

    a. 12 pencils
    b. 5 pencils
    c. 9 pencils
    d. not here

7. Which of the following problems best tells the story of this number sentence? $5 + 2 = 7$

    a. John is 7 years old. His sister is 2 years old. What is the difference in their ages?

    b. There were 7 students in chess club. Then 2 more students joined. How many students belonged to chess club in all?

    c. There are 5 students in John's class who have pets. The other 7 students do not have any pets. How many students are in John's class?

    d. not here

8. Which of the following problems best tells the story of this number sentence? $12 - 6 = 6$

    a. Rick scored 6 points in the basketball game. Serene scored 6 points, too. How many points did they score together?

    b. Mom bought a dozen eggs. She used six of them for breakfast. How many eggs were left?

    c. There are 12 students in room 3. Six students from room 4 join them for math class every day. How many students are in room 3 during math class?

    d. not here

9. Which of the following problems best tells the story of this number sentence? $48 + 7 = 55$

    a. Tojo is thinking of a number that has a 5 in it and is 7 more than 48. What is the number?

    b. The Lollipops scored 55 points in the last half of their game and had 48 points in the first half. How many points did they score in the game?

    c. Forty-eight students signed up for summer camp. Seven students were absent on the first day. How many students came to camp?

    d. not here

Practice Skills: MEASUREMENT AND GEOMETRY

Expectation: Tell time to the nearest half hour. Compare the size of objects. Describe and classify geometric shapes (circle, triangle, square, and rectangle).

Tip: To help you understand the concepts of geometry, put shapes together and take them apart to form other shapes. To help you tell time on a clock, practice counting by fives.

Choose the best answer.

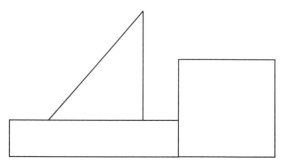

1. What shapes are in this picture?

    a. two triangles and 1 square
    b. 2 squares and 1 triangle
    c. 1 rectangle, 1 circle, and 1 triangle
    d. 1 triangle, 1 rectangle, and 1 square

2. How many sides does a rectangle have?

    a. 3
    b. 2
    c. 5
    d. 4

3. How many sides does a triangle have?

    a. 3
    b. 4
    c. 2
    d. 5

4.   Which figure contains 2 triangles?

a.   b   c.   d.

5. Which item contains a pair of circles?

a.   b.   c.   d.

6. Which figure has a rectangle as its face?

a.   b.   c.   d.

7. How many corners does this figure have?

     a. three
     b. four
     c. five
     d. six

8. How many faces does this figure have?

     a. three
     b. four
     c. five
     d. six

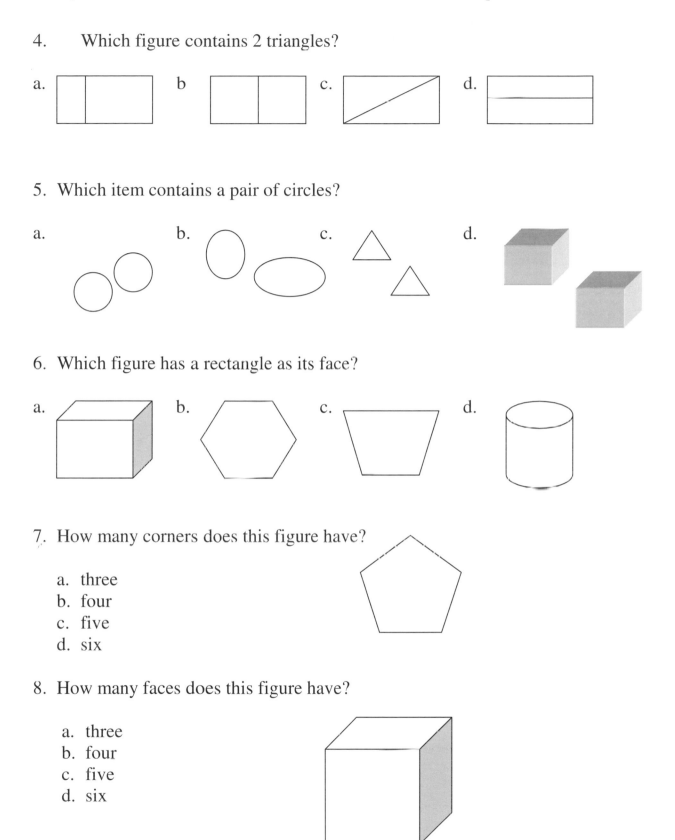

9. If you measure the chalk against the arrows, about how long is the chalk?

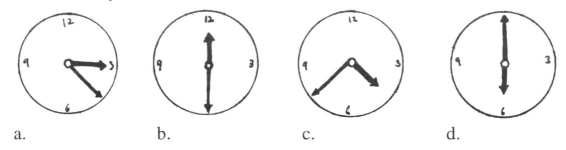

   a.   2 units
   b.   3 units
   c.   4 units
   d.   not here

10. Which clock says 6:00?

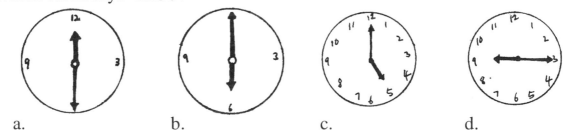

   a.   b.   c.   d.

11. Which clock says 12:30?

   a.   b.   c.   d.

   The students in Oak Street School will have their pictures taken on Friday morning. The students in grade 1 will have their pictures taken at 9:00. The students in grade 2 will have their pictures taken a half-hour later. The students in grade 3 will meet for pictures at 10:00. Kindergarten students will have their pictures taken from 10:30 – 11:30.

12.   Which grade will take the longest to have their pictures taken?

       a. grade 1   b. grade 2   c. grade 3   d. Kindergarten

13.   Which grade will have its pictures taken before the second grade?

       a. grade 1   b. grade 2   c. grade 3   d. Kindergarten

Practice Skill: STATISTICS, DATA ANALYSIS, PROBABILITY

Expectation: Identify patterns. Organize and compare data.

> Tip: In grade one, students are asked to organize items in different ways. Students will use graphs and charts to clarify and compare data.
>
> When reading graphs and charts, start by looking for titles and labels. If you read across the top or bottom of the chart, what do you see? If you read down the sides of the chart, what do you learn? To locate exact information, touch the column lines and row lines with your fingers and follow them. This will help you avoid careless mistakes.

Use the chart to answer the questions.

Results of Student Voting on School Mascot

	Ms. Jay's Class	Mr. Lee's Class	Mrs. Gold's Class	Total
Tiger	ℍ҉	III	III	
Cougar	IIII	II	III	
Turtle	I	II	I	4
Cowpoke	II	IIII	III	9

1. How many students voted for a tiger to be the mascot?

    a. 5
    b. 10
    c. 11
    d. 13

2. How many students in Mrs. Gold's class voted for a turtle as mascot?

    a. 1
    b. 2
    c. 3
    d. 4

3.   What suggestion received the most votes?

     a.   Tiger
     b.   Cougar
     c.   Turtle
     d.   Cowpoke

4.   What suggestion received the least number of votes?

     a.   Tiger
     b.   Cougar
     c.   Turtle
     d.   Cowpoke

5.   Whose class liked the Cowpoke mascot the best?

     a.   Ms. Jay's class
     b.   Mr. Lee's class
     c.   Mrs. Gold's class
     d.   all of the above

6. How many more students voted for a Tiger than for a Cougar?

     a.   2
     b.   11
     c.   5
     d.   1

7. Whose class had the most students vote?

     a.   Ms. Jay's class
     b.   Mr. Lee's class
     c.   Mrs. Gold
     d.   all of the above

8. Whose class had 10 students vote?

     a.   Ms. Jay's class
     b.   Mr. Lee's class
     c.   Mrs. Gold's class
     d.   all of the above

9. What comes next in the pattern?

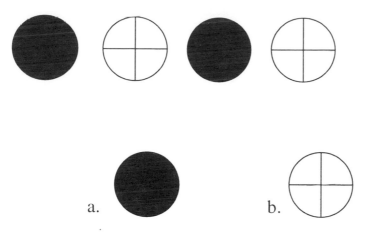

a.   b.

10.   What comes next in the pattern?

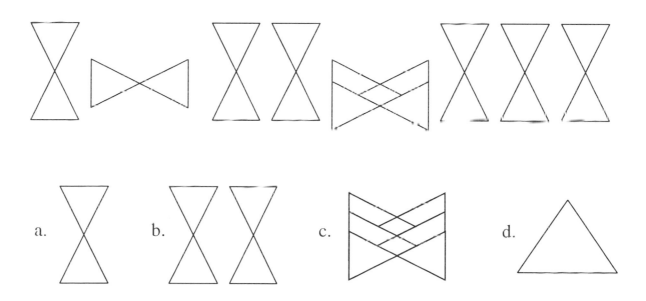

a.   b.   c.   d.

Practice Skill: MATHEMATICAL REASONING

Expectation: Read and solve simple mathematical situations.

Tip: When trying to solve a word problem, read through the entire problem carefully. Look for key words when deciding the best way to solve a problem. (Addition words – in all, altogether. Subtraction words – how many more, how many fewer, how many left.) After solving the problem, read the question again and double check to make sure that your answer makes sense with all the information given in the problem.

ACTIVITY # 1 - Read each problem and choose the number sentence that best solves the problem. If the correct answer is not one of the choices, choose "d. not here."

1. Michele has 8 dog stickers. She has 9 cat stickers. How many more cat stickers than dog stickers does she have?

   a. $8 + 9 = 17$ more dog stickers
   b. $8 + 9 = 17$ more cat stickers
   c. $17 - 9 = 8$ more cat stickers
   d. not here

2. Jenny is 8 years old. Sasha is 5 year older than Jenny. How old is Sasha?

   a. $8 - 5 = 3$ years old
   b. $8 + 5 = 13$ years old
   c. $8 + 8 = 16$ years old
   d. not here

3. There are 44 boys in the first grade at Coldwater School. There are 52 girls attending first grade there. How many students are there in Coldwater's first grade?

   a. $44 + 52 = 96$ students
   b. $52 - 44 = 8$ students
   c. $44 + 8 = 52$ students
   d. not here

4. Victor is six years younger than Jorge. Jorge is 15 years old. How old is Victor?

   a. 15 + 6 = 21 years old
   b. 21 – 15 = 6 years old
   c. 15 – 6 = 9 years old
   d. not here

5. Ten students were eating lunch at one side of a table. Two more students sat next to them. There were nine students sitting at the other side of the table. How many students were eating lunch at the table?

   a. 10 – 2 = 12 students
   b. 10 + 9 = 19 students
   c. 10 + 2 + 9 = 21 students
   d. not here

6. Simon has 4 pens. Beth has 3 more pens than Simon. Abby has 2 more pens than Beth. How many pens does Abby have?

   a. 4 + 3 + 2 = 9 pens
   b. 4 + 7 + 9 = 20 pens
   c. 4 + 1 + 3 = 8 pens
   d. not here

7. There are 12 students in room 3. Six students from room 4 join them in math class every day. How many students are in room 3 during math class?

   a. 12 + 3 + 4 = 19 students
   b. 3 + 6 + 4 + 3 = 16 students
   c. 12 + 6 = 18 students
   d. not here

ANSWER KEY - MATH

Basic + Facts	**Basic – Facts**	**Number Sense**
Exercise # 1	Exercise # 1	Exercise # 1
1. D	1. C	1. B
2. A	2. B	2. D
3. A	3. A	3. D
4. B	4. C	4. B
5. A	5. C	5. A
6. B	6. C	6. C
7. D	7. D	7. B
8. C	8. A	8. D
Exercise # 2	Exercise # 2	9. C
1. D	1. C	10. A
2. A	2. A	11. C
3. D	3. D	12. C
4. D	4. B	13. B
5. A	5. A	14. B
6. D	6. C	15. A
7. B	7. A	16. C
8. C	8. B	17. A
9. B	9. D	18. C
10. C	10. B	19. B
11. B	Exercise # 3	20. A
12. A	1. B	21. B
Exercise # 3	2. C	22. A
1. C	3. B	23. B
2. D	4. D	24. B
3. B	5. B	25. B
4. A	6. C	26. B
5. C	7. C	27. A
6. B	8. B	28. A
7. A	9. B	29. B
8. D	10. C	30. B
9. C	Exercise # 4	31. B
10. B	1. D	32. A
Exercise # 4	2. B	33. A
1. A	3. C	34. B
2. B	4. D	35. A
3. C	5. B	36. A
4. D	6. D	37. B
5. A	7. C	38. B
6. D	8. D	
7. D	9. B	
8. A	10. A	
9. C		
10. C		

Number Sense
Exercise # 2
1. A
2. C
3. D
4. B
5. A

Exercise # 3
1. A
2. B
3. D
4. A
5. C

Exercise # 4
1. B
2. B
3. B
4. C
5. B

Number Sense
Exercise # 5
1. C
2. B
3. C
4. A
5. A
6. C
7. B
8. C
9. C
10. A

Algebra & Functions
1. A
2. B
3. C
4. C
5. B
6. C
7. D
8. B
9. A

Measurement & Geometry
1. D
2. D
3. A
4. C
5. A
6. A
7. C
8. D
9. B
10. D
11. A
12. D
13. A

Statistics, Data
1. C
2. A
3. A
4. C
5. B
6. A
7. A
8. C
9. A
10. C

Mathematical Reasoning
1. D
2. B
3. A
4. C
5. C
6. A
7. C

NOTES

HISTORY - SOCIAL SCIENCE

Practice Skill: COMMUNITIES AND CITIZENSHIP

Expectation: Understand your role and the roles of others within your community.

> Tip: Students in grade one learn about the rights and responsibilities of citizenship. They think about the factors that affect life in their own neighborhoods and compare their lives to those of people who lived many years ago.

Choose the best answer for each question.

1. Good citizenship at school means _____.

   a. following school rules
   b. being kind to others and using good manners
   c. playing fair at recess
   d. all of the above

2. Your neighbors are always part of your _____.

   a. family
   b. community
   c. fire department
   d. time line

3. An example of a service provided by your community is _____.

   a. post office or mail delivery
   b. trash pick-up
   c. police and fire protection
   d. all of the above

4. People who help their community by providing services for free are called _____.

   a. volunteers
   b. relatives
   c. senators
   d. employees

Practice Skill: RESOURCES

Expectation: Identify and know the value and uses of resources.

Tip: We are rich with resources in our country. That is, we have many things that our people can use to meet their needs in life. We have vast human resources (smart, creative, talented, and hard-working people to provide us with goods and services) and enormous natural resources that provide us with food, fuel, and shelter.

Choose the best answer for each question.

1. Which of the following things is <u>not</u> a natural resource?

   a. fresh water
   b. forests
   c. good soil
   d. money

2. Which natural resource do we use to run our cars?

   a. wood
   b. animals
   c. oil
   d. coal

3. Which statement about resources is <u>not</u> true?

   a. Trees give us shelter, food, and fuel.
   b. Water gives us something to drink and provides us with electricity.
   c. Water is a resource that is never harmful to communities. We can never have too much water.
   d. Oceans contain fish, a source of food.

4. What is a good way to save our natural resources?

   a. Use less electricity and water.
   b. Wash glass containers and use them over again.
   c. Take part in a recycling program so that old things can be turned into new things.
   d. all of the above

Practice Skill: MAP READING AND GEOGRAPHY

Expectation: Use map skills to locate specific locations.

> Tip: If you have trouble remembering directions, use this trick. Think about a clock face, but instead of the numbers at the quarter hour (12, 3, 6, and 9), substitute the letters N, E, S, and W. To remember which letter goes where, start at the top and say to yourself, "Never Eat Soggy Waffles!"

Exercise # 1 - Choose the best answer for each question.

1. The United States is a _____.

    a. city
    b. country
    c. continent
    d. river

2. The two oceans that border the United States are _____.

    a. Canada and Mexico
    b. Europe and Asia
    c. Pacific and Atlantic
    d. Gulf of Mexico and Indian

3. We live in the _____ of California.

    a. country
    b. town
    c. state
    d. city

4. Which countries are our neighbors?

    a. Europe and Asia
    b. North America and South America
    c. Australia and China
    d. Mexico and Canada

Exercise # 2 - Choose the best answer to each question. As you answer each question, label the map to learn about JoJo's community.

JoJo's Community

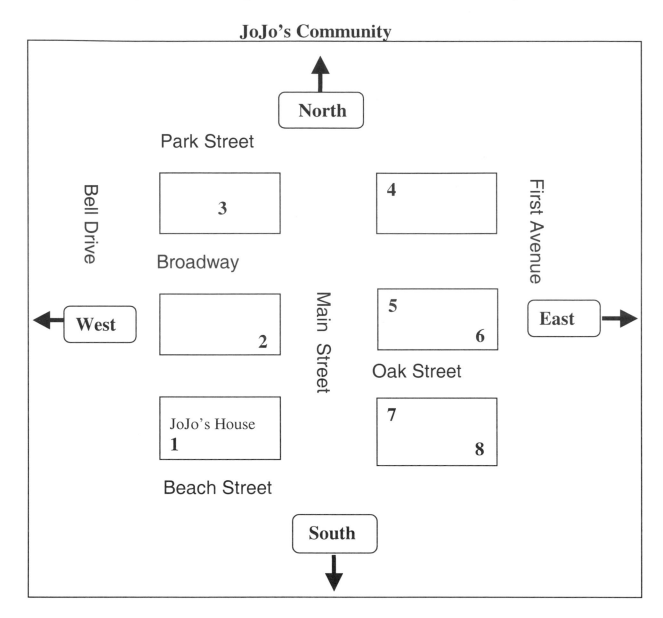

1.   JoJo lives at # 1 on the corner of Beach Street and Bell Drive. JoJo lives in what part of his community?

    a.   north or northeast
    b.   south or southwest
    c.   east or southeast
    d.   west or northwest

2.   There is a very large park in JoJo's community. JoJo walks his dog there every day. From his house, JoJo walks north on Bell Drive. He crosses Oak Street and Broadway, and he is there. The park is _____ on the map.

    a. # 3
    b. # 2
    c. # 7
    d. # 2

3. JoJo's dad works at the fire station. To get there from home, he goes east on Beach Street and north on First Avenue. The station is on the corner of Oak Street and First Avenue. The fire station is _____ on the map.

    a. # 2
    b. # 4
    c. #6
    d. #7

4. JoJo's mom works in the library. The library is near the fire station. It is located on the corner of Main Street and Broadway. The library is _____ on the map.

    a. # 4
    b. # 5
    c. # 6
    d. #8

5. JoJo's school is north of his house and east of the park. It is bordered by Main Street on the west, First Avenue on the east, Park Street on the north and _____ on the south.

    a. Broadway
    b. Oak Street
    c. Bell Drive
    d. Beach Street

6. Using the information given in exercise 5 above, JoJo's school is _____ on the map.

    a. # 2
    b. # 3
    c. # 4
    d. # 5

7. JoJo must travel _____ to go from his school to his house.

    a. north
    b. south
    c. west, then north
    d. east

8. JoJo's grandparents live at _____ on the corner of First Avenue and Beach Street.

    a. # 1
    b. # 2
    c. # 7
    d. # 8

9. Every Saturday morning, JoJo goes to his grandparents' house. Without crossing any streets, they all go to the post office. They walk west on Beach Street and turn the corner to go north on Main Street   They stop at _____, the post office on the corner of Oak Street and Main Street.

    a. # 2
    b. # 5
    c. # 6
    d. # 7

10. From the post office, they cross Main Street and head north. They cross Oak Street. They stop at the store on the corner of Oak Street and Main Street to buy ice cream. The store is _____ on the map.

    a. # 2
    b. # 5
    c. # 6
    d. # 7

11. The park is _____ of the school.

    a. north   b. south   c. east   d. west

12. The library is _____ of the market.

    a. north   b. south   c. east   d. west

ANSWER KEY
HISTORY-SOCIAL SCIENCE

Communities & Citizenship
1. D
2. B
3. D
4. A

Resources
1. D
2. C
3. C
4. D

Maps & Geography
Exercise # 1
1. B
2. C
3. C
4. D

Exercise # 2
1. B
2. A
3. C
4. B
5. A
6. C
7. B
8. D
9. D
10. A
11. D
12. C

NOTES

SCIENCE

Practice Skill: PHYSICAL SCIENCE

Expectation: Understand basic principles about matter.

> Tip: Students in grade one learn about matter, how it can change forms, and how it moves. Everything around us is matter in one form or another: our toys, our food, our water, and even the air that we breathe. Anything that takes up space is matter.

1. Matter that flows and takes the shape of its container is _____.

   a. ice cream
   b. liquid
   c. solid
   d. gas

2. Matter that has its own shape and keeps that same shape when it is moved is _____.

   a. water
   b. liquid
   c. solid
   d. gas

3. Matter that does not have its own shape and spreads out to fill its container and take its shape is _____.

   a. furniture
   b. liquid
   c. solid
   d. gas

4. Which statement is true about matter?

   a. Air does not take up any space.
   b. Matter does not change its shape or temperature.
   c. Heat can melt some solids.
   d. Solids never change into liquids.

5. An example of a solid is _____.

    a. honey
    b. vinegar
    c. banana
    d. bubbles in a soft drink.

6. When a liquid _____, it changes from liquid to a gas.

    a. evaporates
    b. melts
    c. freezes
    d. cools

7. When a solid _____, it changes to liquid form.

    a. evaporates
    b. melts
    c. freezes
    d. cools

8. An example of friction is _____.

    a. rubbing your hands together
    b. light shining through a window
    c. when a shadow is formed
    d. when a paper clip touches a magnet.

9. An example of force is _____.

    a. a prism
    b. a rainbow
    c. a shadow
    d. a pull

10. Which statement is true about magnets?

    a. They are all the same strength.
    b. They are pieces of metal that attract other pieces of metal.
    c. They are all the same shape.
    d. A magnet's force can not pass through another object.

Practice Skill: LIFE SCIENCE

Expectation: Know the similarities and differences of animals and plants.

> Tip: In grade one, students learn about plants and animals and how they stay alive in the different places where they live.

1.   An example of a nonliving thing is _____.

   a.   a bug
   b.   a bush
   c.   water
   d.   an ant

2.   Which statement tells about nonliving things?

   a.   They need air and light.
   b.   They need water and food.
   c.   They breathe, grow, and change.
   d.   They can move or they can be moved.

3.   An example of a living thing is _____.

   a.   water
   b.   grass
   c.   rock
   d.   dirt

4.   In a plant, the _____ keeps the plant in the ground and takes in water.

   a.   stem
   b.   flower
   c.   trunk
   d.   root

5. Which part of the plant makes the food for the plant?

   a. leaves
   b. roots
   c. item
   d. flower

6. One of the main differences between plants and animals is that

   a. animals need to eat food, but plants make their own food when sunlight hits their leaves.
   b. animals move, but plants do not move.
   c. animals grow, but plants do not grow.
   d. animals need water, but plants do not.

7. Which kind of animal has three body parts and six legs?

   a. reptile
   b. amphibian
   c. bird
   d. insect

8. Which kind of animal feeds milk to its babies and has hair or fur on its body?

   a. reptile
   b. amphibian
   c. mammal
   d. bird

9. The only animals that have _____ are birds.

   a. two legs
   b. feathers
   c. two wings
   d. gills

10. _____ are animals that do not have any bones.

    a.   mammals
    b.   birds
    c.   amphibians
    d.   insects

11. A _____ is a larva.

    a.   caterpillar
    b.   butterfly
    c.   wing
    d.   frog

12. When a young frog hatches out of an egg it is a _____.

    a.   bullfrog
    b.   insect
    c.   reptile
    d.   tadpole

13. Which habitat covers three-fourths of the world?

    a.   forest
    b.   rain forest
    c.   ocean
    d.   desert

Practice Skill: EARTH SCIENCE

Expectation: Know about the weather, the seasons, and the water cycle.

Tip: In first grade, students learn about weather: how it can be observed, described, and measured.

---

1.   A person who studies the weather is called a _____.

        a.   airologist
        b.   meteorologist
        c.   windman
        d.   thermometer

2.   When we want to measure how hot or how cold something is, we use a _____.

        a.   scale
        b.   ruler
        c.   thermometer
        d.   clock

3.   Wind is _____.

        a.   moving air
        b.   clouds
        c.   electricity
        d.   always cold

4.   Clouds are _____.

        a.   white air
        b.   gas
        c.   tiny drops of water
        d.   icycles

5.   The water cycle includes _____.

        a.   windmills
        b.   wheels for traveling from one place to another
        c.   water moving from the Earth to the sky and back again.
        d.   all of the above

6.   Which term is <u>not</u> part of the water cycle?

        a.   reflection
        b.   evaporation
        c.   condensation
        d.   precipitation

7.   When water evaporates, it heats up enough to change from water into
        _____.

        a.   raindrops
        b.   snow
        c.   hail
        d.   water vapor

8.   When water condenses, it _____.

        a.   warms enough to change from water into water vapor
        b.   cools enough to change from water vapor to drops of water.
        c.   magnetizes to form lightning.
        d.   only happens in the spring.

9.   Which season has the least number of hours of sunlight?

        a.   fall
        b.   winter
        c.   spring
        d.   summer

ANSWER KEY
SCIENCE

Physical Sciences
1. B
2. C
3. D
4. C
5. C
6. A
7. B
8. A
9. D
10. B

Life Sciences
1. C
2. D
3. B
4. D
5. A
6. A
7. D
8. C
9. B
10. D
11. A
12. D
13. C

Earth Sciences
1. B
2. C
3. A
4. C
5. C
6. A
7. D
8. B
9. B